ISLAM IN VICTORIAN LIVERPOOL

ISLAM IN VICTORIAN LIVERPOOL

AN OTTOMAN ACCOUNT OF BRITAIN'S FIRST MOSQUE COMMUNITY

Yusuf Samih Asmay

Translated and edited
with an Introduction and Appendixes by
Yahya Birt, Riordan Macnamara
and Münire Zeyneb Maksudoğlu

CLARITAS
BOOKS

1 2 3 4 5 6 7 8 9 10

CLARITAS BOOKS

Bernard Street, Swansea, United Kingdom
Milpitas, California, United States

CLARITAS
BOOKS

First Published in May 2021

Typeset in Adobe Garamond 14/11

Islam in Victorian Liverpool
An Ottoman Account of
Britain's First Mosque Community

By Yusuf Samih Asmay

Translated and edited
with an Introduction and Appendixes by
Yahya Birt, Riordan Macnamara
and Münire Zeyneb Maksudoğlu

A CIP catalogue record for this book is available from the British Library

ISBN: 978-1-80011-982-6

DEDICATIONS
786

To my dearest Fozia and my wonderful
children, Sulayman and Layla, thanks for all
your support, patience and love

To my dear wife Emna and wonderful children Selma and Maryam.
To the unknown Victorian convert.

To Husameddin, thanks for
your love and support
To my dear parents, thanks for instilling in me linguistic passion
and work ethics

Yahya Birt is a community historian who has taught at the University of Leeds. He has an M.Phil. in Social and Cultural Anthropology from the University of Oxford. He has published over a dozen peer-reviewed articles on Islam in Britain and co-edited *British Secularism and Religion: Islam, Society and State* (Markfield: Kube, 2016). He lives in West Yorkshire with his family and two cats. He likes walking and being grumpy about the state of the world. He can be reached on Twitter @ybirt.

Riordan Macnamara is a Senior Lecturer at the Institute of Cultural and International Studies, University of Paris Saclay. He is researching Islam in Victorian England and the processes of religious conversion, identification, adaptation and transmission at the Liverpool Muslim Institute for the University of Bourgogne, France. He lives with wife and children in Yvelines, France. He doesn't tweet.

Münire Zeyneb Maksudoğlu is a PhD student of Early Modern Studies at the University of Sussex. Her research is focused on Renaissance Drama in conjunction with Anglo–Ottoman relations. She lives in Brighton with her husband. She likes solitary walks and railways.

CONTENTS

APPENDIXES

ABBREVIATIONS

AH	Anno Hegirae ("in the year of the Hijra")
BOA	Başbakanlık Osmanlı Arşivi
IW	*The Islamic World*
LM	*Liverpool Mercury*
LMI	Liverpool Muslim Institute
LPRO	Liverpool Public Records Office
TC	*The Crescent*

TIMELINE OF THE KEEP–ASMAY CRISIS

1895

FEB

Nafeesa Keep arrives in Liverpool from America; later employed as an editor on *The Crescent*

JUN

11	Crown Prince Nasrullah Khan of Afghanistan arrives in Liverpool as part of official visit to Britain
12	Nasrullah visits the LMI and donates £2500
13	Nasrullah leaves for London; sometime after this date, Keep writes to Nasrullah in London criticizing the LMI, which Barakatullah and Quilliam find out about later
14	Outgoing Liverpool Consul Kenan Bey writes highly critical briefing of the LMI to Ottoman ambassador in London, Rüstem Paşa
22	Quilliam and Barakatullah journey to London to aid Nasrullah
29	Quilliam and Barakatullah spend the weekend with the Crown Prince

JUL

3	Nasrullah visits Queen Victoria at Windsor Palace
4	Quilliam and Barakatullah return to London to assist Nasrullah daily at Norchester House

1896

JAN–MAY

Asmay's account serialized in pro-Young Turk newspaper in Egypt; published as book, *Islam in Liverpool*

JUN

22   LMI annual meeting when the fullest rebuttal of Asmay's book is given, but also some of his reforms are adopted

1898

MAY

2   Quilliam has private audience with Abdulhamid II at Yildiz Palace, who affirms his continued support for the Liverpool Muslims, according to *The Crescent*

31   Asmay's *Islam in Liverpool* banned by the Minister of the Interior within the Ottoman domains

INTRODUCTION

Exposing the Sheikh: Yusuf Samih
Asmay and the Liverpool Muslim Institute

YAHYA BIRT, RIORDAN MACNAMARA
AND MÜNİRE ZEYNEB MAKSUDOĞLU

William Henry Abdullah Quilliam (1856–1932) was arguably the most prominent figure in nineteenth-century Islam in Britain. He declared his conversion publicly in 1887 and then for the next twenty years preached Islam in Liverpool, attracting hundreds of people to convert to Islam. He established the Liverpool Muslim Institute, centred around Britain's first attested mosque community; our current knowledge is that earlier prayer spaces in Britain were informal, ephemeral or private, serving Muslim sailors, students, diplomatic missions or embassy staff, or servants in the country homes of Anglo-Indian colonial families. At first, this fledging community struggled with local hostility and even violence at times, but it persevered to gain a measure of civic recognition within Liverpool as well as prominence in the Muslim world. In part, this was due to the sensational novelty of a Muslim convert community born in the second port, Liverpool, of the world's greatest empire of the day. However, this novelty was skilfully exploited by Quilliam, both a journalist and lawyer by training, through the production of over 800 weekly issues of *The Crescent* between 1893 and 1908, which made the Liverpool Muslim Institute known in the East.

Until very recently, scholarship on the Liverpool Muslim Institute has relied heavily on Quilliam's own publications to account for his life and that of the small Liverpool Muslim community. Asmay's unique account, based on a 33-day research visit to Liverpool for which he deployed observation, interviews and post-visit correspondence, gives us a contemporary outsider's view of Britain's first mosque community, and one of impressive rigour notwithstanding the mistakes and misunderstandings within. His travelogue not only provides invaluable insights into Quilliam's character but also into the everyday worship and religious practices of the Liverpool Muslim Institute, which was still at a relatively early stage in its development

1

when it reflected significant religious syncretism between Protestant Christianity and Sunni Islam. Asmay does much to bring the Liverpool Muslim Institute as a transitional, hybridised institution between Christianity and Islam into proper focus for the first time. He also provides eloquent witness to the great success that Quilliam's propaganda had in the Muslim world and just how far and wide news of the Liverpool Muslim Institute had spread in its heyday.

Pressure to embody or somehow represent their faith when in England marks out Muslim travelogues to colonial Britain, both before and after this unique text of 1896. Asmay's account gives us a somewhat of a respite from Orientalism and what Claire Chambers calls "reverse-Orientalism"[1] and instead allows us to eavesdrop upon the great Muslim debates about political and religious revival at the apogee of European colonialism but one conducted right at the margins of the *umma*, in a fledging micro-community of converts in Victorian Liverpool of all places. Yet the success of Quilliam's propaganda turned this seeming marginality on its head to create Liverpool as an Anglophone nexus for pan-Islamism not just in the Muslim world but uniquely to the Muslim subjects of the British Empire itself, spread by print and steamship through its maritime trading routes.

The bulk of this introduction will set out and engage with the context for Asmay's text, picking out its most significant insights, before considering the refutation of the travelogue by the Liverpool Muslim Institute in 1896, and its subsequent banning by the Ottoman authorities in 1898. This is preceded by giving some background on Asmay himself.

Who was Yusuf Samih Asmay?

Yusuf Samih (d.1942) was born in Adana in modern-day Turkey. After completing his studies at the Köprülüoğlu Madrasa, Istanbul, he was appointed to an Ottoman-run school in Tanta, Egypt, as a Turkish-language instructor. Samih published his first work in 1885, *al-Arif Kalfa*, a Turkish–Arabic grammar book. Under his new penname of Asmay (Asmāʿī/Asmaî), after the Arabic philologist and grammarian (740–828), he penned *El-Esâs*, a Turkish grammar compendium for Arabic speakers.

---

1 C. Chambers, *Britain Through Muslim Eyes: Literary Representations, 1780–1988* (Basingstoke, UK: Palgrave MacMillan, 2015), p.46.

Picture 1: Yusuf Samih Asmay (d.1942)

In the 1890s, British-occupied Cairo, secured by a large garrison, attracted foreigner traders. The capital was home to the largest population of Britons in Egypt, with over 6000 residing subjects[2] that tended to form an exclusive, self-segregated community, disinclined to mingle with the other groups of colonial British subjects, and much less so with the native Egyptians.[3] Evelyn Baring, the agent and consul-general in Egypt from 1883 to 1907, epitomises the mindset of most English residents in Cairo, his words allowing the modern reader to fathom the divide between Egyptian ethnic groups, and Asmay's encounters, as an Ottoman, with the British occupier. Claiming to understand the internal mindset and religious outlook of the "Oriental", the consul writes:

> The Englishman came to Egypt with the fixed idea that he had a mission to perform.... But [he] will find, when he once applies himself to his task, that there is a thick mist between him and the Egyptians.... Consider the

---

2 M. Deeb, "The Socioeconomic Role of the Local Foreign Minorities in Modern Egypt, 1805–1961", *International Journal of Middle East Studies*, 9, 1978, p.16. This figure excludes other groups of British imperial subjects.

3 H. Bowman, *Middle East Window* (London: Longmans, Green & Co., 1942), p.140.

mental and moral attributes, the customs, art, architecture, language, dress, and tastes of the dark-skinned Eastern as compared with the fair-skinned Western. It will be found that on every point they are the poles asunder.[4]

This sense of British superiority was not only cultural: it was also engrained in colonial law. In Egypt, foreign residents were granted extra-territorial rights, known as capitulations, that placed them beyond local jurisdiction, leading to a sense of entitlement and, therefore, a persistent awareness on both sides of the British as occupiers.

During the first decades of British occupation, the Egyptian press had become a crucial tool to deploy Egyptian nationalist discourse. The British responded by financially supporting pro-occupation and secular newspapers and periodicals, such as *Al-Muqaṭṭam*. As the latter were also critical of Ottoman central governance, other papers emerged to provide counter-discourses, promoting a nationalistic, pro-Ottoman line. Asmay, as a translator and promotor of Ottoman Turkish as a cen-tralising common language for Ottoman subjects, was concerned about Egyptian media being increasingly published in English, French, Ital-ian, Greek or Armenian. Since the only Turkish–Arabic Egyptian news-paper, *Vekayi-i Mısriyye*, advocating Egyptian autonomy as an Ottoman dominion, had been banned by order of the Khedive (the Viceroy of Egypt), Asmay took the initiative to produce a new pro-Ottoman news-paper *Mısr* from 1889, written in Turkish

Besides journalism and language teaching, Asmay was a keen travel writer, visiting England three times between 1891 and 1895. Reports of his first journey were published in instalments under the name *Seyâhat-ı Asmay* (*Asmay's Travels*), before being published in book form in 1892.[5] Setting off from Cairo to Ismailiya, Asmay sailed up the Suez Canal to Port Said, crossing the Mediterranean, and stopping at Gibraltar before sailing northwards to arrive at Plymouth on England's south coast. Dis-embarking there, he bought a third-class ferry ticket for London, heading up the Channel to the North Sea before sailing up the River Thames. The journey took thirteen days for a sojourn that was to last less than two months. Asmay stayed at the homes of friends and relatives, visiting London, Cambridge and Brighton. In his *Seyâhat*, Asmay depicts the towns he visits and muses on British culture and mores. His travelogue

4 The Earl of Cromer, *Modern Egypt* (London: MacMillan, 1908), Vol. 2, p.144.
5 Y.S. Asmaî, *Seyahat-i Asmaî* (Matbaatülcâmîa: Kahire, 1308AH/1892).

stands out for the severity of his criticisms of the British. For this Ottoman resident of British-ruled Egypt, Britons were hypocritical, conceited and harboured a deeply rooted aversion to Islam.[6] He also discusses various British misrepresentations of Turkey, the Ottoman Empire, and the Islamic faith. During a heated discussion, Asmay blames folkloric Sufism (literally, "dervishness", *dervîşlik*) and its "antics" (*maskaralığı*), and asserts that the reason Muslims have fallen behind the Europeans is the neglect and marginalisation of Sunni orthodoxy in their own societies.[7]

Visiting Europe from an Ottoman domain (albeit one under British control), Asmay was building on the tradition of Ottoman diplomatic travel accounts (*sefaretname*) and, from the mid-nineteenth century, personal non-official travelogues (*seyahatname*). A specific literary genre had emerged with Hayrullah Efendi in the 1860s, a hybrid travelogue combining narratives of travel, musings on European society, rules of Western etiquette, and tips for tourists. A recurring literary technique of the genre was for the Ottoman visitor to feign surprise and bewilderment upon encountering Western societies and mores, a playful clash of cultures intended to arouse the reader's interest.[8]

6 B. Asiltürk, "The Image of Europe and Europeans in Ottoman-Turkish Travel Writing" in B. Agai, O. Akyildiz and C. Hillebrand (eds) *Venturing beyond borders: Reflections on genre, function and boundaries in Middle Eastern travel writing* (Baden-Baden: Ergon Verlag, 2013), p.43.

7 For a translation into modern Turkish of Asmay's *Seyahat*, see F.N. Şahin, *Yüzyildan Bir Osmanli Seyahatnamesi: Seyahat-i Asmaî* [*An Ottoman Travels over the Century: Asmay's Travels*], unpublished MA Thesis, Dept. of History, Marmara University, 2010.

8 Examples include the travelogues of Ottoman official Abdülhak Hâmit in Paris (1876), London (1886) and the Hague (1895), or the more pro-Western Ahmet Midhat Efendi's travelogue to Europe, published in 1891–2, in which the author advocates for Ottoman adoption of Europe's "material progress" without harming Ottoman ethics, customs and lifestyle, or being plagued by Europe's "moral decadence". There was also Ahmet İhsan's tour of Europe, published in instalments in the avant-garde journal he founded, *Servet-i Fünun* (1891), then in book form in 1892, after having received permission from the Ottoman Ministry of Education; see Asiltürk, *op. cit.*; P. Dumont, "De Constantinople à Constantinople: la traversée de l'Europe par les voyageurs ottomans à l'âge de l'Orient-Express" in *Les formes du voyage: Approches interdisciplinaires* (Strasbourg: Presses universitaires de Strasbourg, 2010). Ahmet Ihsan's traveling companion was none other than Lütfi Simavi Bey, who was on his way to Liverpool to take up the role of Ottoman Consul General (1891–3), where he encountered Quilliam and the LMI, reporting back to the Porte. For details on Lufti Bey's relationship with the LMI, see C. Bayindir, *İsmail Lütfi Bey (Simavi), Ve Liverpool Başşehbenderliği* [*Mr. Ismail Lütfi (Simavi), Liverpool's Ottoman Consul-General*], unpublished MA thesis, Dept. of History, Mimar Sinan Fine Arts University, Istanbul, 2019.

The present text is Asmay's second travelogue.[9] Unlike his 1891 journey to England, he returned in 1895 with the stated purpose of visiting the Liverpool Muslim Institute led by Abdullah Quilliam. This Liverpool sojourn was published in instalments in a short-lived Egyptian pro-Young Turk periodical, *Basîr al-Sharq*, run by a certain Rashid Bey.[10] It was then published in book form in 1895–6 (1313AH) and went through at least two impressions.

In Cairo, Asmay published several Turkish treaties on religion and society that he had translated into Arabic. His most political statement was to publish the *Mes'ele-i Şarkiyye* (1900) by Mustafa Kamil Paşa (1874–1908), the Egyptian nationalist, journalist and lawyer, and founder of both the anti-British newspaper *Al-Liwā'* in 1899 and the National Party (Al-Ḥizb al-Waṭanī) in 1907.[11] For Mustafa Kamil, it was crucial that the Egyptian Khedivate and Ottoman Turkey agree on the treatment of the British as unlawful occupiers, and that if the Porte accepted British colonial rule, the prospect of Egyptian national independence would be lost.[12] Asmay also translated and published a general treatise on Islamic law (*El-Ihticab*, 1900) and a defence of the Islamic veil, both by the Ottoman Sheikh al-Islam Abdullah Cemaleddin b. Hasan Şemseddin (1848–1917), who was then the cabinet minister in charge of religious and legal matters in Istanbul and an important Sufi figure in the Ushshākiyya (Uşşâkiyye) Order. Asmay's

---

9 The title was clumsily translated on the front page as *The Islam at Liverpool* (*Liverpool Müslümanlığı*), which we have rendered as *Islam in Liverpool*.

10 L. Hirsowicz, "The Sultan and the Kheldive, 1892–1908", *Middle East Studies*, 8/3, Oct. 1972, pp.287–311 (p.301).

11 During Asmay's visit to Liverpool, Mustafa Kamil was in Toulouse, France, to deliver a speech against British occupation of Egypt. He said, "We are not hostile to Europeans, nor to anyone. We are truly hostile to British occupation and we say it loud and strong. We have been waiting for England to liberate us for thirteen years now. [...] It is not our fault if England has not yet understood the necessity to evacuate.... We firmly believe that it is our right and duty to come [to Europe], after so much patience, and demand the freedom of our country and enlighten the minds about everything that is going on in our homeland.... It is the moral interest of Europe to return Egypt to herself and to prove, by such a glorious act, that she hears the cries of an unjustly oppressed people." See M. Kamel [*sic*], *Conférence sur l'Egypte* (Toulouse, 1895), pp.17–19. That Asmay translated and published his writings in 1900 points to his approval at that time of Kamil's perspective on the need to oust the British from Egyptian politics, and that British rule in Egypt hindered integration of traditional Islamic values around the Ottoman caliphate combined with European social and industrial advances.

12 For Mustafa Kamil's reception in French intellectual circles, see J. Adam's preface to his *Egyptiens et Anglais* (Paris: Perrin, 1906), pp.5–19.

final travelogue was to Sicily (*Sakılye Sicilya Hatırası*, 1920). His *Yazımız* (1927) was a defence of the use of Arabic script in Turkish in the run-up to Ataturk's legal imposition of Turkish alphabet Romanization the following year. Asmay died in 1942 in Egypt.

Asmay's Arrival in Liverpool

When Yusuf Samih Asmay came to Liverpool in July 1895, the LMI had just bid farewell to Nasrullah Khan (1874–1920), the son of Afghanistan's Amir Abdur-Rahman, who had been installed by the British Crown following the Treaty of Gandamak. The young Crown Prince had been officially invited to England by Queen Victoria in his father's stead, as Abdur-Rahman was too ill to travel. The prince and his entourage of forty were greeted with formal honour and decorum at the Liverpool Muslim Institute. Before leaving, he donated £2500. According to Asmay's account, Quilliam promised the Prince to spend the money on a purpose-built mosque named after him to which he stipulated that it should be given the Amir's, his father's, name, and not his own. *The Crescent*, which recorded that the sum was given to Quilliam in the form of two bags of gold, gave Quilliam more latitude for the gift "to be used by him in such manner as he might think best for the promotion of Islam in Liverpool."[13] This gift allowed for a full refurbishment of the LMI, but also furthered suspicions over possible financial embezzlement by Quilliam. Asmay echoed and added to these accusations. With this donation came an expose that was potentially life-threatening for the LMI. At the 1896 annual meeting, Quilliam provided a lengthy audit in order to refute these accusations directly, which was published in *The Crescent* (see excerpts in Appendix 2).

As a Cairo-based Ottoman, Asmay was familiar with the imperial politics of intrusion and interdependence. He would have understood the Khan's gift as a political manoeuvre serving the purpose of aligning the interests of both countries, manifested by the Khan's pecuniary involvement in the emergence of a British-led, Anglophile Muslim movement. The Afghan Amir was staunchly opposed to the industrialisation of his country, which he saw as Western cultural intrusion. In his welcoming speech to Nasrullah (delivered in English, and in Persian translation by Maulana Barakatullah), Quilliam wove the imperial metaphor of "the sun of reason is darting its rays on the West, while the East is enveloped

13 *TC*, 08/07/1895, p.7.

by the shades of tradition and imagination", so that "steps should be taken to follow in the wake of Great Britain in matters of new sciences and arts".[14] Quilliam was taking a political position in favour of imperial British investment in Afghanistan.

In recounting the Prince's visit to the mosque in Chapter 5, Asmay does not take a clear political position, but highlights the discrepancies between the Khan's favourable impressions of an orthodox Western Islamic movement and his own critical conclusions that the LMI was an unorthodox "fictitious thing". In doing so, Asmay was indirectly undermining both the terms of this renewed partnership between the British Empire and its Afghan protectorate, and Quilliam's interest in receiving recognition as "Sheikh al-Islam" from the Afghan court. Quilliam's strategic goal was to bolster his own position as a mediating religious authority ("the Sheikh-ul-Islam of the British Isles") between the British Empire, its Muslim protectorates and their subjects, and the independent Muslim states, the most important of which were the Ottoman domains.

Asmay and Nafeesa Keep: The Institute's critics united

One of the first LMI members to engage in conversation with Asmay was Nafeesa Mary T. Keep, an American convert who had arrived in Liverpool six months earlier (see her profile in Appendix 3). Asmay's English was not that proficient, so Keep, who spoke French, acted as his translator. Keep had a history of confrontation with male authority figures in America that preceded her sojourn in Liverpool. She was more learned in Islamic legal rulings (*fiqh*) than most converts of her generation and had developed stronger principles of Islamic orthodoxy than her convert counterparts at the LMI. During Asmay's stay, she wrote a letter of complaint to Sultan Abdulhamid II, probably with Asmay's aid, via the Liverpool Ottoman Consul, Tahsin Bey, heavily criticising Quilliam and the LMI and expressing her desire to receive financial help to relocate to an Islamic country (see her letter in Appendix 1). Her conversations with Asmay were decisive in persuading him to expose the fraudulence of Quilliam and the LMI, and to see that doing so was a religious duty. By openly voicing these criticisms, Asmay may have inadvertently exposed Keep as a traitor to Quilliam's cause, and she was expelled from the LMI during his visit. At the LMI's annual meeting later that year (see Appendix 2), Quilliam indirectly condemned Keep as "the profligate,

---

14 *TC*, 03/07/1895, p.5.

the traducer, the slanderer and backbiter, the evil-minded, the unjustly suspicious, and the self-aggrandizer", adding that "the place of such an one is not amongst us".

Asmay's Main Criticisms of the Liverpool Muslim Institute

1. Religiously Unorthodox

Asmay is highly critical of the LMI's religious practices. Echoing the concerns of the Liverpool Ottoman Consul,[15] he regards them as a "Quilliamist innovation" (بدئة كوئيليامى), a reprehensible or even unlawful innovation in religion. Further, Asmay uses the term *tarīqat*, or Sufi order, to describe the group formed around Quilliam, which he dubs the Quilliamiyya (طريقت كوئيليامى),[16] thus relating the practices of the LMI converts around their leader as akin to those of a Sufi order and its sheikh. In his *Seyâhat* (1891), Asmay had written that:

> [T]he current state of the sublime Sufi orders has turned into a desert, the sands of time have blown away their old wisdom, so that ingenue spiritual guides and their followers who traverse these paths have gone astray.[17]

For Asmay, a reform-minded Ottoman intellectual, equating the LMI's Islam with a folkloristic Sufi *tarīqat* placed it on the margins of Islam alongside other groups that had strayed from the truth. Where Quilliam saw necessary adaptation to a new, often hostile, context, Asmay saw deviation and delusion. When Asmay explained that a female Muslim convert could not, according to Islamic law, remain married to her Christian husband, Quilliam replied pragmatically that dissolving such marriages was impossible.

For Asmay, as their leader, Abdullah Quilliam was to blame for his group's deviations in worship, with its most visible display of these being the public "Sunday Services". Asmay writes trenchantly that Quilliam had borrowed "from Protestant styles of worship and calls it Islamic

---

15 In a letter from Consul-General Esad Kenan Bey to Rüstem Paça from June 14, 1895. M.A. Sharp, *On Behalf of the Sultan. The Late Ottoman State and the Cultivation of British and American Converts to Islam*, unpublished thesis (2020), pp.64–5.

16 Use of such a term, aimed to be derogatory, was not new. On the opposite side of the spectrum of anti-LMI criticisms, a similar term is used by a visiting missionary in 1891. "It is not Mahommedanism," he writes, "but Quilliamism." J. Monro, *Moslems in Liverpool* (Calcutta: Joseph Culshaw, 1901), p.46.

17 Şahin, p.105.

worship and has made Muslim convert brothers and sisters pray with music for the past eight years, [and] has not taken the right path."

2. The Sunday Services

These public Sunday events can be traced back to the foundation of the Liverpool Muslim Institute in 1887, and were reported by the press, whether British or foreign. "On Sunday evenings," writes a journalist,

> There are two services – one at seven o'clock, to which the general public is admitted, and which is conducted entirely in English, the service consisting of the reading of selections from the Koran and a lecture on some phase of Islam. The second service is held at half-past eight, and is called the "Maghrab Nimaz," [sic] and admission to this service, which is conducted in both Arabic and English, is strictly restricted to the followers of the Prophet. Prior to each of these services the muezzin, or caller to prayers, ascends the balcony, and gives the "Azan," or call to prayers.[18]

This public Sunday service, as noted by other visitors, including Asmay,[19] was in fact a full religious ceremony with an order of service that was "almost exactly as an evangelistic service".[20] It may be noted that the LMI's Sunday evening services took place at the same time as the Anglican Choral Evensong, or Evening Prayer, in Protestant churches across the United Kingdom, i.e. after the evening meal.

By comparing Asmay's description of the Muslim Sunday services with those provided by Clark and Pool, we can adduce the precise order of the eleven distinct elements that made up the service that Asmay attended:[21]

> (1) The muezzin makes the call for prayer in English and in Arabic from the Museum window on the first floor.

---

18 *The Bristol Mercury and Daily Post*, 17/11/1891, p.5.

19 The most detailed accounts, as well as Asmay's, are provided by J. Monro's 1901 pamphlet, preserving earlier missionary reports serialised in 1892 in the *Punjab Mission News* by Dr Henry Martyn Clark, who had visited the Liverpool Muslim Institute in 1891, and J.J. Pool, *Studies in Mohammedanism* (London: Archibald Hamilton, 1892), which seems to be derivative of Clark's more lengthy account in certain particulars.

20 Monro, p.13.

21 An in-depth study of the syncretism of religious practices, mores and identities at the LMI is, at the time of writing, being undertaken by Riordan Macnamara for a research thesis at the University of Bourgogne, France.

(2) The audience then enters the mosque and takes their places, freely choosing their seats. The ladies keep their hats on, and the men may don fezzes provided at the entrance. Three women, who make up the choir, sit next to the organ.

(3) On the stage, the organist sits at the organ and starts playing a "voluntary".

(4) The presiding chair[22] comes solemnly out from the ablution room[23] on to the stage with the lecturer, both wearing dark red fezzes.

(5) Upon their entrance, the assembly rises and sings the *Fātiḥa* in the way of an Anglican anthem.[24] Still standing, they all then sing a hymn from their Hymnal.[25] These hymns, written by Nonconformists or Anglicans, were well-known to the congregation, convert or Christian, although some dogmatic Christian elements had been expunged by Quilliam.

(6) After the hymn, the assembly sits. The presiding chair, still standing, delivers an *extempore*, a spoken prayer from the Prayer Book,[26] that Asmay

22 Called "the Chair" or the one that "presided" in *The Crescent*, the "imam" by Asmay. In Anglican Evensong services, the one leading liturgy is the "officiating minister", the "celebrant".

23 In a Protestant church, the equivalent of the LMI ablution room is the sacristy, where the minister dresses, washes his hands, says a prayer and from where he or she proceeds to the altar. The use of the ablution area as sacristy is yet another example of elaborate religious syncretism at the LMI.

24 The LMI Hymn Book names this Qur'anic chapter (*sūra*) a "chant" and divides each verse into shorter portions, separated by a "pipe", i.e. " | ", so it is likely that the *Fātiḥa* was delivered by the assembly in the manner of an Anglican chant. In Anglican mass, the Lord's Prayer is recited upon the entrance of the celebrant.

25 In this case, the LMI Hymn Book was the equivalent of the *Book of Common Prayer* in Anglican Evensong.

26 The prayers were collected in a booklet that has yet to be found. The only reference to this "Prayer Book" is in Monro, pp.9–10. It can be assumed that the content was very similar to the one compiled by convert Hamid Snow, leader of an associated Anglo-Islamic group in India (H. Snow, *The Prayer Book for Muslims* (Lahore: The Mohammedan Tract and Book Depot, 1893)). For Clark, the LMI prayers from the Prayer Book are "a queer medley, with almost nothing of the Mahommedan about them. They are wholly modelled on the form of Christian prayers.... One sentence ran 'teach us to love one another'. Another petition is that they might 'rejoice with them that do rejoice, and weep with them that weep....' In another prayer they confess themselves to be 'defiled with the exceeding sinfulness of sin'; for 'all, like sheep, have gone astray.'" "It is such a prayer," adds Pool, "as is heard doubtless every Sunday in a Unitarian Church." (Pool, p.399).

associates with an Islamic *du'a'*. Another hymn is then sung from the hymnal, the number being called by the chair to the assembly. Once again, the hymn chosen is a popular Protestant one, with a familiar musical arrangement. At Asmay's service, more than one hymn was sung, the author expressing surprise at having to stand up and sit down so frequently.

(7) The officiant reads from the Qur'an in English.[27]

(8) A hymn written by Quilliam is sung by the choir of three female converts.

(9) Then, the "lecture"[28] is given from the stage by the lecturer. It is likely these were the "lectures" advertised at 7pm on Sundays in *The Crescent*. In Asmay's account, the lecture that Sunday was given by Haschem Wilde, who challenged Christianity and promoted Islamic superiority over the Christian faith. However, these lectures frequently covered a variety of topics not related to religious belief.

(10) After the lecture, a hymn composed by Quilliam is collectively sung, before the saying of a final grace: "The peace of God which passeth all understanding, and which the world can never give, keep you, Amen."[29]

(11) Similar to the Protestant mass, the organist plays out the congregation, and a copy of the latest issue of *The Crescent* is handed out to attendees on their way out.

After attending the service, Asmay classes it as non-Islamic and an unsanctioned innovation (*bid'a*) in worship. He equates the mosque to a music "salon", and describes the congregational singing with interest and amusement, comparing one of the hymns performed to a Parisian music-hall duet that he had seemingly enjoyed when in the French capital. He enjoys singing along, although he admits facetiously to getting an elbow jab from the attendee sitting next to him for his poor singing.

It is the second Sunday "service", only accessible to Muslims, that triggers Asmay's urge to defend the principle of religious orthodoxy.

---

27 At this precise juncture in the English Protestant mass there would be a reading from the Bible.

28 Called "address" (Pool, p.399), "sermon" (Monro, p.13) or "*khuṭba*" (Asmay).

29 Monro, p.15.

Announced in *The Crescent* as the "Isha Namaz" (*ṣalāt al-ʿishā'*) prayer that takes place on Sundays after the 7pm public service, he attends with higher expectations. In a sarcastic tone, Asmay decries the lack of Islamic authenticity in the evening prayer he witnesses. He notes that nobody has performed the Islamic ritual ablutions properly, that the women occupy the first row, keep their brimmed hats on, and nod their heads to indicate prostration. Wearing fezzes, the men sit behind the women out of a sense of propriety. Asmay notes that although the orthodox prayer direction towards Mecca is respected, the standard prayer times are not. He notes that the "Isha Namaz" is set at a fixed time, rather than moving earlier or later according to the seasonal length of the day. Asmay notes that the fixed time for "Isha" throughout the year causes a great deal of misunderstanding amongst foreign Muslim visitors. On occasion, they came to pray at the time of *maghrib* prayer (three cycles of prostration) only to find themselves performing the longer *ʿishā'* (four cycles) before its time instead. For an educated and practising Sunni Muslim such as Asmay, this was a line that ought not to be crossed, as it contradicted essential elements of the inviolable five daily *ṣalāt*.

3. Anti-Christian Polemics

Asmay disapproves of the lecture delivered by Haschem Wilde. According to *The Crescent*, the speech was a success: "Fully one half the number in attendance were strangers, who listened with unabated interest to the able discourse."[30] However, Asmay thought it was unabashedly anti-Christian, causing some Christian attendees, he notes, to get up and leave during the speech, with "Quilliam's group publicly uttering such views that neither Islamic books nor Islamic scholars express, using such strong language against Christianity [that] will bring more harm than benefit." Asmay's opinion that these attacks on Christianity were detrimental to Muslim–Christian relations echoed similar concerns raised by the Liverpool Consul Kenan Bey only a month earlier: "instead of striking a conciliatory tone in order to dispel erroneous ideas Christians have in general of Islam," the diplomat writes to his superior Rüstem Paşa, "the members [of the LMI] constantly attack Christianity, and so feed the antipathy that pushes that religion away from ours.".[31]

Asmay asked Wilde for a copy of his lecture, probably in order to

---

30 *TC*, 24/07/1895, p.57.
31 14/06/1895, BOA. HR.SFR.3 446/50, in Sharp, pp.67–8.

quote parts of it in his account. The lecturer refused to give it to him. His refusal lends credence to the argument that the content of *The Crescent* and *The Islamic World* was carefully curated and that the converts were aware of the importance of disciplined communication in the Institute's periodicals to keep control over their public image.

4. The need to regulate the Institute as an endowment

Asmay was critical of the LMI's organisational structure. He pointed out that, "[t]he structure that they have built does not resemble ours.... Mr. Quilliam has set off to do it as he thought most fitting and in accordance with his own customs, but without consulting Islamic scholars or literature." Crucially, for Asmay, the LMI should have been created as a charitable institution, a *waqf*, i.e., an endowment that perpetually reserves a founder's property for designated persons or some private or public objects, and is managed accordingly.

Although the LMI did claim to have a "Muslim legal scholar" in the person of Barakatullah Bhopali, Asmay thought him unworthy of occupying this dignified position. Asmay did not consider Barakatullah to be a qualified Islamic scholar, even though the Maulana had trained as an *'ālim* at the Madrasa-i-Sulaimanya in Bhopal, India. Regarding the LMI's structure, the young Indian believed that the Institute being open to the public was enough for it to be considered a *waqf*. Contrasting the LMI to Leitner's exclusive mosque in Woking, he writes that "a mosque, according to Islamic laws, is public property (wagf [*sic*]) to which every believer has free access".[32] Whether the LMI belonged to or was managed by an Islamic institution or was a place owned and led by Quilliam is an issue that Barakatullah did not address.

The practicalities of establishing an Islamic *waqf* in Victorian Britain, organised and managed by the Porte through its Consulate in Liverpool, were conveniently left unaddressed by Asmay. His concerns were not about the feasibility of such a project. Rather, his goals were to assess, criticise and, if necessary, expose. By reasserting that the political and religious leader of the Islamic World was the Sultan, and that the LMI should integrate with the orthodox Islamic *modus operandi* as a *waqf*, Asmay aims to debunk the possibility of an English-led Islamic group

---

32 Quoted by J. Gilham, "Professor G. W. Leitner in England: The Oriental Institute, Woking Mosque, Islam and Relations with Muslims, 1884–1889", *Islam and Christian-Muslim Relations*, 2020, p.19, DOI: 10.1080/09596410.2020.1851932.

operating beyond the pale of Ottoman control and authority in the name of an untamed pan-Islamism. For him, the pivotal centre of Sunni Islam was Istanbul; whatever British Islam was, or might become, it should remain subordinate to the Ottoman centre.

5. A British-led Islam?

According to Asmay, instead of conforming to existing religious and political Islamic structures, Quilliam was developing a separate pan-Islamic network from Liverpool that lacked legitimacy. This assertion was not new. Prior to Asmay's visit, Quilliam's motives had been debated among Cairo's intellectuals. For some, the LMI was yet another sly British gambit, a political attempt to undermine Islamic unity through propaganda about an English mosque with Muslim converts to buttress Britain's imperial authority and subjugate Egypt's colonised Muslims. For these detractors, the LMI's hidden aim by associating Islam with Britishness was to counter Islam as a unifying anti-colonial force and to assimilate Muslims as imperial subjects. For an anonymous writer in Ahmad Urabi's anti-British newspaper *Al-Ustadh*, the Institute was no more than a "political mosque located in Liverpool, the one built and made popular by the colonialists of Egypt, to deceive the Egyptians." He added that, "It is better for you to chop your hand off than to place it in the hand of the [British] foreigner."[33] Other Egyptians defended Quilliam as "honest" and the LMI as "praiseworthy", calling on the Islamic principle of withholding judgment, that "there is no duty on us to judge others except by what is apparent". The famed Egyptian reformer Rashid Rida even asked the same question of his teacher, Muhammad Abduh, to which the latter responded that the Liverpool mosque was not a political manoeuvre but genuinely Islamic as it had grassroots origins.[34]

While he does not mention this debate in his home city of Cairo, it seems unlikely that Asmay was oblivious to it. As can be seen in his first chapter, he had followed news reports about the Liverpool Mosque closely, hearing "news of reservations from certain persons who deserve to be called precautious rather than nit-pickers" and suggestions that Quilliam

---

33 Translated by A. Abouhawas in "An Early Arab View of Liverpool Muslims: *Al-Ustadh* and Sheikh Abdullah Quilliam between Accusation and Exoneration during the Age of British Imperialism", *EveryDay Muslim*, 04/03/2020, https://www.everydaymuslim. org/blog/an-early-arab-view-of-liverpools-muslims/, accessed 14/12/2020.

34 Idem, citing I.A. 'Adwī, *Rashīd Riḍā, al-Imām al-Mujāhid* (Cairo: Mu'asasat al-Miṣ-riyya al-'Āma li-Tālīf wa l-Anbā' wa l-Nashr, 1964), A'lām al-'Arab, Vol. 33, p.96.

had converted for financial gain.

During his visit, Asmay came to suspect that Quilliam's motives had a political element. Like Quilliam, Asmay was a journalist and newspaper editor, and was well aware of the influence of print and its importance in the creation and transmission of new collective identities.[35] Asmay understood that Quilliam saw *The Crescent* as the means by which he could propagate the idea of a unified, British-led Islam:

> In the whole world, according to Mr. Quilliam, it is only the publications of this printing press [in Liverpool] that will gather the ideas of Turks, Arabs, Persians, Indians, Afghans and other nations of Islam in one place thus making them one family. By its newspapers promoting the idea of Islamic unity all Muslims will be gathered under Quilliam's banner, so that they will politically prevail over other nations.

Asmay writes that he immediately disagreed with Quilliam's scheme, pointing out to him that the unifying language of Islam was Arabic and that the only legitimate leader could be the Ottoman "caliph of the prophet of the Lord of the Worlds".

Quilliam's Character in Question

In Chapter 5, Asmay critically assesses Quilliam's leadership of the LMI as well as his personal integrity. Asmay does not hold back in exposing what might be described as Quilliam's "feet of clay", i.e. his personal shortcomings. A psychoanalytic comparison of contemporary religious teachers who fall short of their own teachings is suggestive when considering Quilliam's case. They share biographical elements and traits with Quilliam like an only childhood, precocious talent and focus on creative or intellectual pursuits, the discovery of a spiritual truth after illness, personal charisma, a gift for public speaking, an intensity of conviction that attracts followers, and a fondness for elitism while paying lip-service to accountability. The question Asmay raises is whether Quilliam also had feet of clay too, and fell prey, like some other religious leaders do, to thinking that the rules or principles he taught his followers did not really apply to him. This exceptionalism, redolent both of Thomas Carlyle's

---

35 For the classic statement on the central role of the print media in creating modern collective identities such as nationalism, see B. Anderson, *Imagined Communities: Reflections on the Origin and Spread of Nationalism* (London: Verso, 1983/2006).

'prophet as hero' and of what Asmay more trenchantly dubs hypocrisy, can be manifested by religious leaders with "feet of clay" in three ways: (i) love of wealth – being entitled to special privileges so they do not have to worry about money, often ending up living in luxury; (ii) love of sex – breaking the rules of sexual propriety they impose on their followers, often by the seduction and even abuse of followers who trust them as spiritual guides; and (iii) love of power – the exploitation of their followers, most commonly by delegating their chores to followers, so they do not have to deal with trivia, or, more seriously, the manipulation of followers' gullibility for amusement or sadistic motives.[36]

The salient insight from Anthony Storr's psychoanalytical framework is how it links ideas of exceptionality, something that can be seen in Quilliam's self-image and self-presentation as Islam's founding figure in Britain (with the conversion stories of the early converts echoing those of the Prophet's Companions in Mecca), and its connection with personal moral failings in terms of money, sex and power. This is not to suggest for a moment that Quilliam should be pre-emptively diagnosed as a textbook case; nonetheless, the moral failings that Asmay alleges warrant an assessment through this approach as potentially instructive. The moral failings highlighted include examples of all three categories, namely, the embezzlement of charitable monies, adultery and sexual conquest, and the exploitation of followers in painting a full picture of the LMI as a beacon of Islam in Britain through his publications, while in fact pursuing fame, fortune and the fairer sex. Some of the salient examples of each are discussed in more detail below.

Yet, despite his moral condemnation of what he sees as Quilliam's personal misconduct, Asmay's proposed solutions are rather modest and pragmatic: namely, that the LMI should be run more transparently and that Quilliam and his family should continue to head the institution within a more rigorous structure modelled on Ottoman regulations for charitable endowments.

1. The Crescent as Propaganda

The crux of Asmay's complaint is that *The Crescent* and, to a lesser extent, *The Islamic World* both project an exaggerated and at times false picture of the LMI and its president. This disillusionment for some visitors from

---

36 A. Storr, *Feet of Clay: A Study of Gurus* (New York: HarperCollins, 1997), Introduction.

the East was not uncommon when they saw how Brougham Terrace appeared rather dishevelled and small in comparison to Quilliam's ebullient prose describing it as a powerhouse of pan-Islamism in the Christian West, and a beacon of hope for colonized Muslims everywhere, which they had read and taken at face value over the years.[37] A more charitable reading would argue that Quilliam talked up his mission to give confidence to those around him and to garner support from others, which was understandable considering how isolated and unsupported the Liverpool Muslims were in their earliest years. In any case, considering that Quilliam published thousands of pages over two decades, checking for internal inconsistencies or corroborating claims from external sources where available is a work in progress. Therefore, a sober final assessment of the veracity and sobriety of *The Crescent*'s entire run is not something that can be attempted here. Instead, we will look at some of Asmay's specific and serious allegations about Quilliam.

2. Embezzlement

Asmay charges Quilliam with running the LMI as a pious fraud to extract thousands of pounds from gullible Muslims in the East for personal profit. The pieces of evidence that Asmay brings together to prove this are firstly negative: the lack of auditing and public accountability of the Institute's finances, and Quilliam's evasiveness when asked directly about it. In and of themselves, these are not evidence of embezzlement but, charitably speaking, could be read instead as signs of informality and even of some amateurism in the running of the Institute in its first decade.

More substantive, however, are the specific allegations that Asmay cites, taken from a local satirical newspaper, *The Porcupine*. Asmay also cites letters he received from LMI affiliates: an anonymous senior member who confirms the allegations of large unaccounted-for donations and embezzlement, and Barkatullah's second letter to Asmay, denying any involvement in financial issues. It must be assumed that Asmay had put the allegations directly to Barakatullah in correspondence; in response, the Maulana did not deny them but disavowed any knowledge or responsibility for the Institute's finances, saying they were in Quilliam's hands. It may well be that self-preservation was at play as Barakatullah

---

37 A. Husain (ed.), *Mian Fazl-i-Husain: Glimpses of Life and Works, 1898–1936* (Lahore: Sang-e-Meel Publications, 1995), pp.85–7; M.H. Kidwai, *Islam in England* (Lucknow: Newul Kishore Press, 1929), pp.2–3.

appeared to be placating both sides. He was later appointed to audit the Institute's 1895–6 accounts under Quilliam's direct instructions. A few months after the audit, Barakatullah left the LMI.

3. Polygamy, Womanizing and the Camden Street Brothel

Asmay does not attack the institution of polygamy itself in his criticism of Quilliam's two marriages, but rather questions them on other grounds. The first is that polygamy was illegal in Britain, and that it was not fit for any Muslim to ignore the law of the land. On top of that Asmay disparages Quilliam's second unofficial marriage under Islamic law to Mary Lyon because of the absence of legal guarantees for her inheritance should he die before her. This had probably been divulged to Asmay by Nafeesa Keep, who had recently lectured at the LMI on this matter.[38] Finally, Asmay worries that to promote and practise polygamy was to compromise the call to Islam in Britain by arousing the suspicions of local women about their unequal status and rights in the faith compared with those of men. There are also claims that can neither be substantiated nor disproven that Quilliam was an inveterate womanizer who had numerous adulterous affairs. When Asmay came to Liverpool in 1895, this was widespread gossip. However, there is some evidence that Quilliam may have owned a hotel that operated as a brothel. As this is a bold claim, it needs to be discussed and treated at length by considering the available primary sources on the matter.

Asmay's claim is that Quilliam was the owner of the American Temperance Hotel at 3–5 Camden Street in Liverpool, which was managed by a couple named Mr and Mrs Cuss, who will be described in more detail below. The scandalous element was that they secretly ran it as what was then called "a disorderly house" or brothel. When the brothel was uncovered by the police, Asmay further alleges that Quilliam acted to ensure the Cusses were not found guilty in court, an endeavour which he failed in, as both were sentenced for brothel-keeping. He did succeed, Asmay avers, in narrowly escaping being charged for the same offence.

A seemingly unrelated claim Asmay makes is that Quilliam ran a private detective agency under the pseudonym of Mr. Victor. The alleged agency investigated family-related cases such as runaways and adultery, and Asmay reports that it was shut down by the police. This second allegation will be considered insofar as it relates to the question of the

---

38 "The Position of Women under Islamic Law", *IW*, Mar. 1895, pp.342–51.

brothel, given that no independent evidence about the agency has been uncovered so far. It is notable that the hotel-cum-brothel and detective agency stories about Quilliam were also circulating widely in Liverpool when Asmay visited in July and August of 1895.

The questions that arise are as follows. Is there more to these claims than malicious gossip? Was Quilliam the owner of the hotel? How much knowledge of or even involvement with the brothel did he have? If there is any truth to the claim that he owned a hotel that acted as a front for a brothel, what could have been his motives? Why take the risk to his reputation or act so immorally? The available primary sources – local news reports, court records, census and other official data, and local business directories – uncover a tale of highly suspect behaviour but do not give us definitive answers to these questions.

Like many other expanding British seaports in the late nineteenth century, prostitution grew in Liverpool to serve the needs of an estimated 40–50,000 seamen coming in and out of the port every year. It was reported to the House of Commons in 1878–9 that Liverpool had a floating population of around 20,000 sailors at any one time, who would return home cash-laden with backpay to spend on drink and sex, supporting a large economy of pubs, beer houses and brothels around the Liverpool docks.[39] In December 1890, the police carried out a crackdown on the brothels, centring not only on the brothel-keepers but on the landlords or owners of the properties too.[40] All the known brothels at the time, some 342, were prosecuted that same month, and in the first nine months of 1891 there were another 468 prosecutions for brothel-keeping. Two-thirds were fined £5 plus costs (there is evidence the brothel-keepers thought the modest fine a manageable financial risk), while only 5% were imprisoned.[41] In 1891–2, there were 727 prosecutions for brothel-keeping with only 19 of these being successfully applied to owners and landlords.[42] The police attributed the failure to prosecute landlords and owners to the weak legal powers available to them. The written notice

---

39 *Liverpool Courier*, 24/02/1891, p.3; *LM*, 23/05/1878, p.8; T. Hands, *Drinking in Victorian and Edwardian Britain* (Palgrave MacMillan, 2018), Ch. 3: Beyond the Spectre of the Drunkard, https://www.ncbi.nlm.nih.gov/books/NBK524987/.

40 *LM*, 11/12/1890, p.5. Quilliam took three cases defending other brothel-keepers in court during the first wave of the police crackdown: *LM*, 31/12/1890, p.3; 18/02/1891, p.8; 25/02/1891, p.8.

41 *LM*, 30/10/1891, p.6.

42 *LM*, 10/11/1892, p.8.

served by the police to landlords or owners informing them that their premises operated as "houses of ill-repute" had no legal weight, even if the police proved the premises' *subsequent* use as a brothel in the courts. In 1890–1, 639 written notices were served to landlords and owners but only 32 of them were eventually prosecuted.[43] Instead, it was usually the tenants acting as brothel-keepers who were prosecuted rather than their landlords, which has implications for how we might understand the trials involving the Cusses as tenants who named Quilliam as their landlord.[44]

The American Temperance Hotel was caught up in February 1891 in the police's crackdown on brothels; the police had observed "on various dates disorderly women entering the house in the company of different men".[45] Eliza Cuss was found guilty of brothel-keeping at the Liverpool Police Court the following month and fined £5 with costs. During the trial, it emerged that she had been fined in Manchester for brothel-keeping and selling liquor without a licence in 1875.[46]

It was only during the second trial in July 1891 of Mr and Mrs Cuss for ongoing brothel-keeping that Quilliam's involvement in the case became apparent. Quilliam hired an "esteemed friend"[47] of his, a noted lawyer and politician, to defend the Cusses. Dr Andrew Commins (1829–1916) was MP for South Roscommon in the British Parliament and a local councillor for Liverpool's Vauxhall ward for Irish Home Rule, and had trained at Lincoln's Inn and worked the Northern Circuit. If Quilliam was indeed the owner of the hotel as the Cusses told the police in Asmay's account (see Chapter 5 below), then why did he choose to back his tenants in court by hiring and instructing a prominent lawyer on their behalf?[48] After all, Eliza Cuss had already been found guilty of running the hotel as a brothel and of running another brothel in Manchester sixteen years earlier. One reason may have been that George F. Cuss, who

43 *LM*, 30/10/1891, p.6.

44 All Asmay's allegations about the hotel-cum-brothel and the detective agency come in Chapter 5 below.

45 *Liverpool Courier*, 24/02/1891, p.3.

46 For further details of first case, see *LM*, 24/02/1891, p.8; *Liverpool Courier*, 24/02/1891, p.3; *LM*, 03/03/1891, p.8; *Litchfield Mercury*, 06/03/1891; and for the previous convictions of Eliza Cuss (then Mitchell) in Manchester see, Calendar of Prisoners, Liverpool Assizes, County of Lancaster, 30/03/1892, LPRO 347 QUA/3/2.

47 *TC*, 21/06/1899, p.389.

48 No property deeds for 3–5 Camden Street, Liverpool, survive from this period; source: Land Registry, telephone interview with Y. Birt, 09/09/2020.

was being charged with brothel-keeping for the first time, was closely associated with Quilliam. He was a convert to Islam from Agnosticism and in 1891 was an LMI official, serving voluntarily as an auditor on the Institute's management team.[49]

During the second trial, the police were called by the prosecution to recount what they had witnessed while keeping a watch on the hotel. Detective-Sergeant Robbins saw known prostitutes entering and leaving the hotel and further noted that George Cuss and one of Quilliam's legal clerks were mounting a counter-surveillance to the police watch.[50] It is reasonable to assume from the presence of Quilliam's clerk that Quilliam wanted to protect the hotel from the police action against it for brothel-keeping, and deputed his clerk to aid George Cuss in keeping an eye on police surveillance of the premises.

The presiding magistrate, A.J. Stewart, was provoked into implying that Quilliam was manipulating the case, and, in making his highly unusual remark (see below), he was likely to have been reflecting the suspicions of the police and the prosecution. The magistrate made this remark when the defence lawyer questioned the probity of the Liverpool police's actions in the case. Dr Commins' concerns centred around Detective-Sergeant Robbins, who had followed one of the women, Florence Harrison, from the hotel back to her lodgings and, between 12 midnight and 1am, asked her to testify for the prosecution. She said Mr Cuss didn't know her when he admitted her into the hotel. When she refused to give evidence, Robbins gave her sixpence as she looked unwell.

Dr Commins submitted that the case had not been proved. He was proud of the character of the Liverpool police, but this kind of prosecution forced on by some goody-goody people would do more harm than good. This sort of thing if pushed too far would introduce corruption in the force. Fancy a man going into a prostitute's room at one o'clock in the morning! That sort of thing would arise out of the police being employed

---

49 There are four references to George F. Cuss as a convert to Islam and LMI member: *Times of India*, 13/11/1891, p.5; U.R. Snow, *The Merits of Islam or the Primitive Faith* (Lahore Mohammadan Tract & Book Depot, 1893), p.6; Monro, p.7; *TC*, 20/11/1907, p.332; for a profile of George Cuss, see Appendix 3.

50 Although the clerk is unnamed in the press reports, it is worth noting that two of Quilliam's legal clerks were Muslim converts and LMI members, one was Thomas Omar Byrne, whom Quilliam was personally close to (see his profile in Appendix 3), and the other was J. Lewis, see *Times of India*, 13/11/1891, p.5.

in the most contemptible of all duties, and he was afraid the bench [i.e. the presiding magistrate] would be corrupted as well as the police. [...]

Mr Stewart.—You may know more about it than I do?

Dr Commins.—Well, that is an observation unworthy of your profession.

Mr Stewart.—I mean from your instructions [i.e. from Quilliam].

Dr Commins.—I repeat that the character of the defence is brought into danger by this act of prosecution, and observations are made from the bench that ought not to be made.[51]

It is noteworthy that Dr Commins did not deny the magistrate's remark but instead called it inappropriate. Nonetheless, A.J. Stewart dismissed the case saying that there was insufficient evidence to show that George Cuss knew he was admitting prostitutes to the hotel.[52] However, the whole affair took a more serious turn the following year.

In February 1892, Eliza Cuss was again charged with brothel-keeping at the American Temperance Hotel in Camden Street at the Liverpool Police Court, with George Cuss charged as an accessory, defended respectively by Dr Commins and Quilliam himself. Eliza Cuss was found guilty, but her sentence was held over for a related case at Liverpool Crown Court. George Cuss was bailed for £50 and later found guilty of brothel-keeping and sentenced "to keep the peace for three months discharged on [his] own recognizance".[53]

Two months later, Eliza Cuss, 45, was charged at the Liverpool Assizes of having conspired with a private detective, Charles Robbins, 32, "to defeat the course of public justice" involving the brothel at 3–5 Camden Street in February 1892. Cuss and Robbins had attempted to bribe a witness for the prosecution, May Hayfield, to leave Liverpool and not take the stand the following day at the magistrate's court, though Hayfield had refused the bribe, even after Robbins offered her money and Cuss offered her a drink. The attempted bribery had taken place at the

---

51 *Liverpool Courier*, 08/07/1891, p.3.
52 Ibid; *LM*, 08/07/1891, p.7.
53 *LM*, 11/02/1892, p.8; 17/02/1892, p.7; City of Liverpool, Quarter Sessions, England and Wales, Criminal Register, 01/12/92, p.62.

Old Pine Apple public house at 2 Camden St., right across the road from the American Temperance Hotel, and had been witnessed through police surveillance. Both were found guilty and sentenced to eight months hard labour, Robbins in December that year as he remained at large and was not caught by the police until August.[54]

As no evidence has been uncovered, it only speculation that Robbins, the inquiry agent involved in attempting to bribe a witness, may have been connected to Quilliam, given that Dr Commins, the defence lawyer previously hired by Quilliam, tried to argue in court that Robbins was not conspiring with Eliza Cuss.[55] There is also the interesting coincidence in Asmay's allegation that Quilliam's private detective agency was shut down by the police in 1891 when he was also under suspicion for his involvement in the Camden St. case.[56] The law was nearly a dead letter when it came to proving knowledge on the part of landlords when it came to brothel-keeping on their premises, so the police and the magistrate could only nurse their suspicions, and could not bring a charge against Quilliam. This may have been what Asmay was obliquely referring to when he mentions that Quilliam "somehow got himself out of this tight corner".

There remains the question of motive. It seems far-fetched, even inexplicable, that Quilliam would jeopardise his public reputation with such a reckless venture, even leaving aside the morality of the issue, which Asmay dwells on at some length in his concluding chapter. We might venture some potential theories here in lieu of anything more concrete. The first is that Quilliam had an overwhelming weakness for women, but did this go beyond his multiple marriages to numerous affairs and assignations as Asmay claimed?

The second theory is a surprising alternative that invites further investigation as our findings here are only preliminary. Quilliam's mother Harriet and his maternal grandfather Dr Burrows were both officials in the national campaign for the repeal of the Contagious Diseases Acts, which was led

54 Calendar of Prisoners, Liverpool Assizes, Country of Lancaster, 30/03/1892 (Eliza Cuss); 05/12/1892 (George Robbins); *LM*, 08/04/1892, p.6; 20/08/1892, p.5; 15/12/1892, p.7; *Liverpool Courier*, 08/04/1892, p.3; 20/08/1892, p.3; 15/12/1892, p.3.

55 *Liverpool Courier*, 08/04/1892, p.3.

56 See the remarks above from the presiding magistrate, A.J. Stewart, in the July 1891 case. More generally, it was common for both lawyers and journalists to hire private detectives at the time (and Quilliam was both), see H. Shpayer-Makov, *The Ascent of the Detective: Police Sleuths in Victorian and Edwardian England* (Oxford: Oxford University Press, 2011), pp.119, 175.

by the feminist Evangelical Josephine Butler (1828–1906) out of Liverpool between 1869–1882. Quilliam's paternal grandfather, Samuel, was also a supporter of the campaign.[57] Thus, the teenage Quilliam was exposed to Butler's radical commitment to gender equality, informed directly by her faith, and also to her distrust of the Church and her commitment to social reform, notably extended to the pastoral care of prostitutes.[58] Camden Street did operate as a "temperance row", as there were three other well-established temperance hotels on the street besides the American Temperance Hotel, and Quilliam had often spoken against the "demon drink" at Camden Hall at 11 Camden St. when it had previously operated as a temperance hall.[59] Is there a direct link between the rescue homes Butler set up for prostitutes in Liverpool in the 1860s, and the temperance hotel-cum-brothel at 3–5 Camden Rd that the Cusses may have ran on Quilliam's behalf? Was there a pastoral motive at play? There is some evidence that Quilliam had pastoral concerns over the treatment of prostitutes and brothel keepers in the opening few months of the crackdown. He argued in court and in front of the Watch Committee, which set policing policy in Liverpool, against the practice of closing brothel houses and merely increasing street prostitution. Instead, he thought that brothel houses could be run quietly in a responsible way. The crackdown would only result in sending prostitutes to "other neighbourhoods or to the workhouse".[60] Or perhaps there was some combination of the two motives: did Quilliam not only share some of W.E. Gladstone's Liberal politics but also his penchant for rescuing fallen women through a mixture of social concern and sexual temptation?[61] Presently, there are no definitive answers about motive but only open questions.

---

57 *LM*, 15/11/1871, p.11; 06/07/1882, p.5; *TC*, 17/04/1901, pp.243–5.

58 For more on Josephine Butler and the Anti-Contagious Diseases Acts campaign see, K. Barry, "Josephine Butler: The First Wave of Protest" in *The Prostitution of Sexuality* (New York: New York University Press, 1994), pp.91–121, http://www.jstor. org/stable/ctt9qg779.7; M. Hamilton, "Opposition to the Contagious Diseases Act, 1864–1886", *Albion*, Spring 1978, pp.14–27, http://www.jstor.org/stable/4048453; H. Mathers, "The Evangelical Spirituality of a Victorian Feminist: Josephine Butler, 1828–1906", *Journal of Ecclesiastical History*, 52/2, April 2001, pp.282–312.

59 *Kelly's Directory of Liverpool & Birkenhead*, Part 1: Liverpool, 1894, p.115; *The Era*, 18/01/1890, p.17.

60 *LM*, 25/02/1891, p.8; *The Examiner*, 24/01/1891, p.5.

61 For Gladstone's social work with "fallen women" and his diary records of sexual temptation, see H.C.G. Matthew, *Gladstone* (Oxford: Clarendon Press, 1997), pp.90–5, reproduced at: http://www.historyhome.co.uk/pms/gladwom.htm, accessed 06/12/2020.

The Politics of Counting Converts

Through Nafeesa Keep, who during Asmay's stay became *persona non grata* at the LMI, Asmay managed to obtain a list of the members who had attended Prince Nasrullah Khan's visit to the LMI a month earlier. The list of LMI members, and therefore the number of converts, had been the object of intense interest from the very beginning of Quilliam's preaching of Islam on British soil. A higher figure would spell success for Islam in England and therefore a threat to Christianity there and throughout the Empire; conversely, a modest number would represent the failure of this first attempt to establish a community of Anglo-Muslims, and proof that the vitality of the competing Christian faith and missions was unchallenged. Quilliam took an active part in this war of numbers and provided an account on a regular basis in *The Crescent*, sometimes mentioning an "allegiance book" into which the newly converted added their names and signatures underneath a declaration of faith. Access to this register became crucial to provide corroboration of Quilliam's claims of conversion, given that donations to the LMI depended on the perception of success, or failure, of this Islamic mission. The Anglican missionary Dr Henry Martyn Clark had visited the Institute four years prior to Asmay's visit with the primary purpose of procuring the register of converts to check Quilliam's public claims about convert numbers.[62] However, Quilliam refused to give him access to the allegiance book, based on protecting the convert's right to discretion in cases where that had been requested. Clark was quick to conclude that Quilliam was lying and that the LMI was a failure, as it served his polemical purposes.

Asmay asked Quilliam how many people he had played a direct role in converting to Islam between 1887 and 1895. Quilliam answered that, while he could not recall the precise figure, it was about 200 in total, and mentioned that the logbook was currently with the Crown Prince in London. Eventually, through Nafeesa Keep, Asmay succeeded in getting hold of a copy of the list it was claimed had been given to the Crown Prince. However, it was certainly not Quilliam's logbook or, as it was often called in *The Crescent*, the "allegiance book".

---

62 H.M. Clark (ca. 1857–1916) was a medical missionary in the Punjab, who trained as a doctor at Edinburgh, graduating in 1892. Born in Peshawar and adopted by the first missionary sent to the Afghans by the English Church Missionary Society, Robert Clark (1825–1900), when his Afghan mother died, he became well-known for his debates with Hindus and Muslims in the Punjab.

When the Amir's son visited the LMI during the summer, quite a few converts were on holiday. Prominent members of the LMI, such as Ali Hamilton or Djemel-ud-Din Bokhari Jeffery who were absent, did not figure in the list. Additionally, as Asmay pointed out, many of the listed members were not converts. Others, like Alfred Quilliam or John Harrison, were in the process of converting. The list lends credence to the notion that LMI aficionados were not required to be Muslim to be granted membership,[63] and that attraction and conversion to Islam could cohabit with a variety of levels of attachment to an individual's non-Muslim cultural and religious background. For many, converting was in fact a simple affiliation, an "alternation"[64] that did not imply a complete disruption of an older identity, discourse or practice. Unlike the way religious conversion was generally understood at the time, conversion was not an unanticipated and individual emotional reset.[65] The conversion offered by Quilliam at the LMI was a *process* of religious adhesion, an adoption of new beliefs and practices alongside older ones, the new and old beliefs and practices fusing together into a synthesis.[66]

Some LMI visitors would have been Victorian cosmopolitans, with an interest in Oriental religions and studies, i.e. what Quilliam had coined "the mysteries of Moslem theology" in 1885 when he was studying Islam but had not yet embraced the faith. Others were simply curious or excited by the subversive novelty of an organised Islamic presence on British soil, and avid to discover for themselves what lay behind the exoticism of England's only self-proclaimed "Church of Islam". The interest of a considerable number of "seekers" at the LMI did not last, with their names frequently appearing and disappearing from *The Crescent*. In any

---

63 Regarding the requirements of LMI membership, although conversion to Islam could be considered as obvious, Asmay's list of members tells us that it was not an obligatory requirement. What is currently known, from Consul Lütfi Bey in 1891, is that a membership fee of five shillings was required, see BOA-Y. PRK, EŞA, 13/88 (bkz. EK-4).

64 For an overview of sociological approaches to conversion, and Travisano's theory of conversion and alternation, H. Gooren, *Religious Conversion and Disaffiliation: Tracing Patterns of Change in Faith Practices* (New York: Palgrave MacMillan, 2010).

65 One of the strong archetypes of religious conversion in the Victorian and Edwardian age was Paul's sudden rapture and conversion on the road to Damascus, see for instance, W. James, *The Varieties of Religious Experience: A study in Human Nature* (New York: Longman, Green & Co., 1902).

66 M.D. Baer, "History and Religious Conversion" in L. Rambo and C. Farhadian (eds), *The Oxford Handbook of Religious Conversion* (Oxford: Oxford University Press, 2014), pp.25–47.

case, religious fluidity was more the rule than the exception. For these reasons, a *current* list of converts at the LMI was onerous to keep, as it could not reflect the fluid, dynamic reality of individual commitment to Islam at the LMI. Quilliam's difficulty in providing up-to-date, accurate totals of existing converts came across in his tendency to pluck round figures out of air when cross-examined by missionaries, journalists or Muslim visitors about the number of converts at the Institute.

Reconsidering Barakatullah in Liverpool

The Liverpool chapter of the precarious, itinerant life of one of the most important pan-Islamists of the early twentieth century, Maulana Bara-katullah Bhopali (1854–1927), has been shrouded in relative obscurity and even speculation, despite interventions in recent scholarship.[67] There was little that could be authoritatively said about the relationship he had with Quilliam or his role in growing the pan-Islamic profile of the LMI community. Asmay's account gives us an entirely new appreciation of the period in showing us that Barakatullah was crucial in using his linguistic skills in Arabic, Persian and Urdu to promote the Institute's profile in the early 1890s to Muslim rulers and philanthropists. This correspondence campaign garnered its greatest success with the Amir of Afghanistan, who recognised Quilliam as the leader of the faithful in England in 1894,[68] and whose son, Nasrullah, as mentioned previously, visited the mosque the following year, gifting it with £2500. In many respects, Barakatullah's two letters to Asmay, reproduced in the text, indirectly lend credence to some of the Ottoman journalist's worst misgivings.

The Keep–Asmay Crisis: Consequences and Significance

It would not be remiss to dub this 1895 imbroglio the Keep–Asmay Crisis, as its chief protagonist and instigator was Nafeesa T. Keep. As her short biography in Appendix 3 shows, Keep was a dauntless, capable personality,

---

67 H. Ansari, "Maulana Barkatullah Bhopali's Transnationalism: Pan-Islamism, Colonialism, and Radical Politics" in G. Nordbruch and U. Ryad, *Transnational Islam in Interwar Europe: Muslim Activists and Thinkers* (New York: Palgrave Macmillan, 2014); M.A. Khan, "Universal Islam: The Faith and Political Ideologies of Maulana Barakatullah Bhopali'", *Sikh Formations*, 10/1, 2014, 57–67, https://doi.org/10.108 0/17448727.2014.888246; S. Siddiqui, "Coupled Internationalisms: Charting Muhammad Barkatullah's Anti-colonialism and Pan-Islamism, *ReOrient*, 5/1, Autumn 2019, pp.25–46, https://www.jstor.org/stable/10.13169/reorient.5.1.0025.

68 *IW*, 18, Oct. 1894, p.189.

fierce in protecting her own rights, a talented foreign correspondent and newspaper editor, a curious intellectual, a good linguist and a competent autodidact in teaching herself about Islam, and, most saliently here, ever willing to stand up to those in authority whom she felt were abusing their position regardless of their public reputation and standing. In all fairness, at times she was also prone to overstating her case in pursuit of a just cause. While it is true that Asmay came to Liverpool with a sceptical frame of mind, he was certainly guided and aided by Keep in coming to draw conclusions about the Liverpool Muslim community and its president that were largely aligned with hers. Keep was certainly as talented and capable as Alexander Russell Webb[69] and Quilliam in writing about, having knowledge of, and showing passion for Islam. As a woman convert who wanted to set up and lead her own Islamic mission in the West, Keep did not receive a fraction of the support and patronage from the Muslim world that her two male counterparts enjoyed.

That said, it was the serialisation and then publication of Asmay's polemical pamphlet that truly precipitated a temporary crisis of legitimacy both for Quilliam and the Liverpool Muslim Institute. It has not yet been considered what Asmay's motives were. Was it simply professional journalistic curiosity combined with Islamic learning and a sense of public duty that propelled Asmay to go to such lengths to examine Quilliam and the Institute's *bona fides* or were there other political or religious agendas at play? Apart from Asmay's opposition to British imperialism in Egypt, shown clearly in his subsequent association with Mustafa Kamil Pasha from at least 1899, we have not been able to uncover any evidence to indicate that Asmay was pursuing an anti-LMI agenda at the time of his visit in 1895.

Asmay was a cosmopolitan intellectual, an Ottoman *madrasa* graduate, translator, publisher, and educator with a journalist's training and curiosity, who lived the bulk of his life in Cairo. He was fluent in Turkish, Arabic, French and Persian, with a passable knowledge of English. Asmay's penchant for travel and travel writing revealed both his instincts to defend the Ottomans and Islam when necessary but also to be open to investigating Europe on its own turf despite having experienced British imperialism at close quarters in Egypt.

---

69 Webb (1846–1916), the first prominent Anglo-American convert to Islam in 1888, a Muslim missionary, diplomat and newspaper publisher. For more on Webb, see the entry on Keep in Appendix 3.

Asmay recognised Western scientific and economic progress but rejected its colonial brutishness and arrogance, and castigated its moral decadence. He stuck to Islamic orthodoxy in religious practice but tolerated an openhanded approach to adapting Islam to European cultural practices and mores. He supported orthodox Sufism over what he saw as its folkloristic antithesis, and orthodox Sunni worship over any application of syncretic practices that he saw in Liverpool. He argued that the LMI should be tied more closely to the caliphate as the centre of governance in Islam and to Ottoman charitable endowment models, yet his critique was initially serialised in a pro-Young Turk newspaper in Cairo.

Thus, the summarising picture that most closely fits the character of Asmay in 1895 is that of an independently-minded Sunni, a loyal Ottoman subject based in British-ruled Egypt with an interest in social and religious reform. As such, it is hard to pigeonhole him as an agent of any major religious or political ideology of the day, although more research needs to be done on his life in Egypt and the intellectual, cultural and political networks he was attached to in Cairo.[70] To the extent that we can judge this matter on the basis of what is currently known, his stated motives may simply have been close to truth of the matter: that he was curious but sceptical about the great publicity the Liverpool Muslims had enjoyed across the Muslim world and wanted to get to the truth. While Asmay was not always successful in his quest and made mistakes at times, which we have noted in the Introduction and in the footnotes to the translation where they arise, he has left a remarkable testimony and analysis of Britain's first attested mosque community.

With the rediscovery, translation and publication of Asmay's *Islam in Liverpool*, it is now possible to see its impact on the Institute. This is most apparent in the reports of the LMI's annual general meetings for 1895 and 1896 (excerpted in Appendix 2), which constitute Quilliam's main responses to Keep in the first year, and to Asmay the following year. While Keep and Asmay are never once mentioned by name and are heavily criticised, nonetheless some of their criticisms clearly were taken on board, whether on a short-term or long-term basis.

---

70 See also Ekmeleddin Ihsanoğlu, *The Turks in Egypt and Their Cultural Legacy* (Cairo: The American University in Cairo Press, 2012), pp.235–237, 251, 310, 351.

1. The Expulsion of Nafeesa Keep

The first ripple effect of Asmay's visit was a notable, immediate focus by Quilliam on bolstering internal solidarity at the LMI with warnings against slander and backbiting. Along with the castigation of the unmentioned Keep as the "profligate, the traducer, the slanderer and backbiter, the evil-minded, the unjustly suspicious, and the self-aggrandiser" at the annual meeting in August 1895, that same summer Quilliam's essay "Al Homazato wal Lomazato (The Backbiter and the Slanderer)" was included in his *Studies in Islam: A Collection of Essays* (1895). In this essay, Quilliam demonstrates with Prophetic traditions from Al-Tabrīzī's *Mishkāt al-Maṣābīḥ* that slander is entirely un-Islamic. He concludes that

> The duty ... of the true Muslim is plain. He is neither to revile his brother believer nor to entertain even a suspicion of him, 'for some suspicions are a crime.' And when calumniated by evil-minded persons, to remember that none have ever entirely escaped calumny, not even the Prophet himself.[71]

Given how successful Asmay was in eliciting damning and sensitive information from other LMI members, it is clear that Keep's expulsion was meant to serve as an example to others, alongside Quilliam's general warning to his community against backbiting and slander.

2. Institutional Reforms

Another effect of the Keep–Asmay Crisis was the publication of a financial account from the LMI's annual meeting in 1895 in *The Crescent*, which had not been done prior to that year. Then, prior to the following annual meeting of 1896, Quilliam received confirmation that Asmay's travelogue was highly critical of him and the Institute, presumably through Barakat-ullah or new LMI member Mustapha Khalil Bey. The core LMI team was mobilised to prepare a major annual report that year that would respond obliquely but substantively to Asmay's criticisms around transparency and accountability. This was published in both *The Crescent* and *The Islamic World*. The 1896 annual report was something of a one-off, as future published reports did not provide such detailed accounts of the Institute's activities for the year and could lack separate audits. Therefore, the Keep–Asmay Crisis cemented the formalisation of the Institute's governance and

---

71 W.H.A. Quilliam, *Studies in Islam: A Collection of Essays* (Liverpool: Crescent Printing and Publishing Company, 1895), p.102.

provided at least the appearance of greater transparency, although run on British associational lines rather than on the Ottoman endowment model that Asmay advocated. The other main effect was that publicised foreign donations to the LMI largely dried up after 1895. Before 1896, Asmay's investigation found that Quilliam received between £7000–11,500 in donations, from Afghanistan, British India (Hyderabad, Bombay and Rangoon), Istanbul and Lagos; Quilliam, when questioned directly by Asmay, only admitted to minor success and great personal expense and inconvenience. According to the LMI's published annual reports, only £41 was received in publicised foreign donations between 1896–1906.[72] The LMI's subsequent campaign to raise £6000 for a purpose-built mosque was a casualty of this diminution in foreign financial support. In 1903, the report of the annual meeting lamented that,

> Some day the Muslim world would appreciate the great mistake they were making in not upholding the hands of the Sheikh in England.... Had the Sheikh been given proper financial aid from the Muslims abroad that he deserved, Islam could have been introduced and secured converts in every large city in the British Isles.[73]

After this mournful complaint, the Institute's finances were no longer mentioned in *The Crescent*'s sporadic reporting of its final annual meetings (1904–8).

72 *LM*, 19/08/1890, p.6; *TC*, 05/08/1893, p.229; 12/08/1893, pp.238–9; 09/06/1897, pp.362–3; 16/06/1897, pp.371–4; 23/06/1897, pp.387–90; 30/06/1897, pp.403–5; 22/06/1898, pp.387–91, 395–6; 29/06/1898, pp.403–7, 410–12; 06/07/1898, pp.419–21; 21/06/1899, pp.387–90; 28/06/1899, pp.403–6; 20/06/1900, pp.387–90; 24/04/1901, pp.259–61; 15/05/1901, p.307; 09/04/1902, p.235; 23/04/1902, pp.259–62; 15/04/1903, pp.235–8; 28/06/1905, pp.403–7, pp.410–14; 18/07/1906, pp.458–9. Basic LMI accounts as part of the annual reports were published in *The Crescent* in 1893, 1896, 1898, 1902 and 1903; accounts were mentioned in published reports in 1890, 1897, 1899, 1900, 1901; accounts and finances not mentioned in published reports in 1905 or 1906; no reports of annual meetings or accounts in 1887–9, 1891–2, 1894, 1904, 1907 or 1908. No extant copies of *The Crescent* for 1894 have yet been found.
73 *TC*, 15/04/1903, p.237.

3. An Argument Within Pan-Islamism

Was there truth behind Asmay's claim that Quilliam pursued a self-conscious ideological project to project a novel form of Anglophile pan-Islamism (with its own idiosyncratic Anglo-Islamic synthesis in worship) globally through print and the imperial maritime routes? Were the contemporary Egyptian concerns, discussed above, about the LMI being a British political manoeuvre to infiltrate and control Islam, outlandish and conspiratorial or did they have some substance to them?

What may have been at play was an argument within pan-Islamism between Asmay and Quilliam, something that his account brilliantly illuminates. As Cemil Aydin argues, pan-Islamism at the end of the nineteenth century was firstly imperial in both its framing and its political impulses in securing political rights – before it later became nationalist and anti-colonial.[74] "Pan-Islamism", as the British coined it, "Islamic unity" as the Ottomans and Asmay termed it or "fraternal union" as Quilliam dubbed it – was invoked within the logic of sustaining imperial order, whether by the British, the Ottomans or the pan-Islamists. The British sought legitimacy in the eyes of its 100 million Muslim subjects as a great pro-Islamic power, while denying Islam itself as a mobilising anti-imperial force;[75] the Ottomans used the language of Islamic unity both to bond its disparate subjects together and to protect Muslims outside of its domains where it could through the limited means of recognition and patronage at its disposal. However, the Sublime Porte did not want to unduly antagonise the British, who had moved away from their alliance with the Ottomans after 1878. What most pan-Islamists shared at the time was a vision that a British–Ottoman concordat could be revived. It was in this strange conjunction of clashing imperial interests that Quilliam's rather novel articulation of pan-Islamist dual loyalty was developed, and was indeed designed to operate within, given that he strove to carve out an authoritative mediating role as "Sheikh-ul-Islam of the British Isles" in the mid-1890s, a position from which both he and his community could benefit.[76]

---

74 C. Aydin, *The Idea of the Muslim World: A Global Intellectual History* (Cambridge: Harvard University Press, 2017), p.231.

75 For more on the imperial promotion of Britain as the "greatest Muhammadan power" see F. Devji, "Islam and British Imperial Thought" in D. Motadel (ed.), *Islam and European Empires* (Oxford: University Press, 2014), pp.254–68, although this was predicated on the British supersession of the Ottomans as the greatest champion of Muslim peoples rather than on rekindling a concordat between the two imperia as Quilliam hoped.

76 Aydin, pp.65–98.

However, Asmay saw dangers in Quilliam's profession of dual loyalty to Crown and Caliph, as a political stance that granted Britain too much legitimacy in its existing imperial domains, which Asmay increasingly wanted to contest in Egypt, as his later involvement with Mustafa Kamil and Egyptian nationalism shows. While Quilliam was famously willing to publicly contest British imperial extension into Sudan in 1896,[77] he offered little criticism of the British in Egypt, which lay at the heart of Asmay's disagreement with Quilliam's form of Anglophile pan-Islamism, whose rationale he expresses most completely in his presidential address at the Institute's 1896 general meeting:

> I believe in the complete union of Islam, and of all Muslim peoples; for this I pray, for this I work and this I believe will yet be accomplished. In England we enjoy the blessed privilege of a free press, with liberty to express our thoughts in a reasonable way, and this advantageous position can be used for the purpose of promoting the entire re-union of Muslim peoples. [...] From Liverpool our steamers and trading vessels journey to each part of the world, and here within the walls of this Institution who knows but that the scattered cords may not be able to be gathered together and woven into a strong rope, *Al-Habbulmateen*, of fraternal union.

Quilliam saw his position in Liverpool as a genuine opportunity, for himself, for his community and for Islam: to advance an Anglophone pan-Islamism centred around the British benefits of freedom of speech and non-sectarian religious freedom. Like his fellow Islamic reformer Asmay, Quilliam thought that the divisions of the *umma* were due to ignorance and backwardness and that the time had come for reason and progress – values that they considered more developed in Western societies – to become the new cement of Islamic belief and society. One Indian Muslim correspondent wrote to *The Islamic World* in February 1895 that:

> It is now time for us to break the spell which held us so long, to unfetter the sweet, seducing charms of fanatical unreason, to gain the solemn march of progress, to eradicate the notion of sectarian differences ... and to unite under the flag of Mohammedan unity.[78]

---

77 R. Geaves, *Islam in Victorian Britain: The Life and Times of Abdullah Quilliam* (Markfield, Leicestershire: Kube, 2010), pp.173–88.
78 *IW*, Feb. 1895, p.310.

Both Asmay and Quilliam believed that the *umma* could use Western advances to its profit, but they clashed over how to bring this about. Despite being marginal Muslim neophytes in a distant imperial metropole, Quilliam assumed that he and other British converts should take a leading role. These white Victorian converts were not only fascinated by the exoticism of non-Christian cultures and traditions, but found the adoption of this oriental otherness more palatable if they could project a rather fantastical form of leadership over non-white Muslims, particularly over Her Majesty's imperial subjects within the imperial British domains. After all, Quilliam's designation as "Sheikh-ul-Islam of the British Isles" came about through nomination by Barakatullah and election by LMI members at a meeting in Brougham Terrace in October 1894; there is no hard evidence to date that the Ottomans ever formally recognised the title or that its officials ever used the title in connection with Quilliam.[79]

In asserting his leadership, Quilliam did not shy away from equating the origins of the Liverpool convert community with the struggles of the first Muslims in Mecca, who were persecuted and marginalised in their own society. In his 1896 annual speech, he makes an explicit parallel between nineteenth-century Liverpool and seventh-century Mecca:

> Just as our glorious Prophet had the assistance of Abu-Bekr, Ali, Omar and Othman, and they were aided by Khaled and Saad, so in this work of planting Islam in England has your president been assisted by Nasrullah [Warren], by Haschem [Wilde], Abdur-Rahman [Holehouse] and many others, and if we are to search for further parallels we can find them between Billal, the first muezzin of Islam, and our own, Hassan Radford, who has frequently in times past boldly given the *azan* amidst a shower of stones flung at him by fanatical giaours.

Quilliam's evocation of Liverpool as Mecca met with strong approval and sustained applause from the assembled LMI members.

Besides the external impact of Asmay's book in the summer of 1896, Quilliam also looked to extend his leadership among Britain's Muslims. In December 1895, a Muslim Capetonian, Mahommed Dollie, an early supporter of Quilliam's, had proceeded to open a mosque in London and

---

79 For an account of the meeting, see 'A Manx Chief of Islam', *Mona's Herald*, 10/10/1894, p.5; for an exhaustive trawl through the Ottoman archives for how Quilliam was actually addressed by Ottoman officials, see Sharp, pp.128–136.

had gained some converts.[80] Like Quilliam, Dollie professed allegiance to the Queen-Empress and advocated for the adaptation of religious practice to English mores and culture.[81] More significantly, two Indian pan-Islamist groups, the Anjuman-i-Islam and the Ikhwan-us-Safa, were actively taking part in religious and political debates from London, and had developed their own connections to the Hamidian Ottoman court at Yildiz Palace. Islam in London was being organised to mobilise resident, non-white Muslims, with whom Quilliam's convert community in Liverpool vied with for legitimacy and leadership.

4. The Departure of Barakatullah

It is safe to assume that the Maulana's departure meant that he was a casualty of the Keep–Asmay Crisis, and that he had outlived his usefulness to Quilliam once he had been ordered to complete the audit of 1896, after his private letter to Asmay was published revealing that he had denied any responsibility for the Institute's finances. It also left the Institute bereft of any in-house ability to conduct direct correspondence campaigns aimed at rulers and philanthropists in Arabic, Urdu or Persian.

5. A Shift Towards Orthodoxy?

Many visitors before Asmay had expressed surprise and scorned the liturgical adaptations put in place by Quilliam. However, the Ottoman journalist was the first to criticise their religious practices in detail for Muslim audiences whose support was essential to Quilliam's credibility, and therefore to the survival of the Liverpool Institute. A substantive and speedy response was required.

In his 1896 report, the LMI's Secretary Omar Byrne did not mention the failure to hold congregational prayers at their canonical times. In-

---

80 *TC*, 10/12/1895, pp.387–8.

81 "Should the Arabic language stand in the way of making converts, I personally ... do not see why we should not have our prayer-books and hymn-books in the English language. Nor would he object to having pews in the Mosque," Dollie writes in *The Crescent* (idem). Dollie was not competing with Quilliam *per se*, at least as far as converting British Victorians was concerned. When a young man, Arthur Ashton, converted to Islam at Dollie's hands, he was asked to send the official declaration of conversion to Quilliam in order for his name to be "duly affixed into the roll-book of True-Believers in England, preserved in the Liverpool Muslim Institute." (*TC*, 05/02/1896, p.508).

stead, he focused on justifying the syncretic Sunday Services. Asmay had been misled by Nafeesa Keep:

> It has been said that these meetings were "Muslim services," and one foolish and ill-informed person in Egypt went so far as to write a ridiculous book, in which he said the English Muslims had an organ in their Mosque and used it in their prayers, and much other nonsense of the same kind. [...] These Sunday meetings are not and have never been considered by us as Muslim services, or used in substitution for the regular prescribed prayers of Islam [...]. They are simply and only Muslim missionary meetings in the fullest extent of the word, and are held in the Lecture Hall of the Institution, specially erected for that purpose. [...] Most of the people in this country are Christians, [...] These people had to be brought gradually into the faith: consequently in order to make them feel more at home at our missionary meetings we held a service something like the one they had been accustomed to in "the days of their ignorance."

Byrne appealed to the early days of Islam to justify these adaptations: the Sunday lectures, that were integrated into the religious services, were a necessity in Victorian England:

> Mahomed used to preach Islam in the streets of Mecca and thus secured some of his earlier converts. Here in Liverpool we know that the first converts were obtained by the means of lectures.

Referring again to the Prophet of Islam, Byrne boldly claims that:

> If the Prophet himself (whose name be forever honoured, esteemed and blessed) were living in Liverpool today, he would approve of everything that our president [Quilliam] has done with regard to this matter.

Quilliam's right to call his people to Islam as he thought best, argued Byrne, was God-given: "William Henry Abdullah Quilliam has been designated by the Almighty to be 'the witness raised up in this land to preach Islam to this people'." In other words, the LMI's Sunday services were not going to be changed on the basis that they were unsanctioned innovations in worship.

Asmay's charges against the heterodoxy of the Friday Prayer were serious. From 1893, *The Crescent* had announced a "Jumma Namaz every Friday at the time of Isha Namaz", i.e. in the evenings, unlike the orthodox time in the early afternoon. From January 1895, the announcement was less time-specific: "Jumma Namaz every Friday." Additionally, for Asmay, this evening get-together was not even an act of collective prayer, and the LMI did not hold a Jumū'a Prayer at all. From his eyewitness participation, Asmay had concluded that, "Wednesdays and Fridays are not for worship but for discussion." It was no longer just a matter of defending Quilliam's inspired choices: the LMI's "Friday Jumma" needed to evolve to counter any backlash arising from Asmay's accusations.

Despite Asmay's claims that Fridays were purely social gatherings, there is evidence that evening Friday prayers were held at the LMI. In 1891, at the height of anti-Muslim attacks on the LMI, it is during the Friday evening "Jumma prayers" that a stranger entered the mosque and threw several black puddings and sausages at the Muslims gathered there.[82] That said, mentions in *The Crescent* of "Jumma prayers" at the LMI mosque were not systematic and tended instead to refer to special events, such as a meeting about the Armenian Crisis (Jan. 1895) or for the anniversary of the Sultan's accession to the throne (Sept. 1895). It is likely that Friday prayers were on hold when Asmay visited, because Quilliam, Barakatullah and Nasrallah Warren were busy in London tending to Prince Nasrullah Khan.

An important consequence of Asmay's criticisms was the progressive development of a Jumū'a Prayer that was more acceptable to orthodox Muslim visitors. One month after Asmay's departure, *The Crescent* and *The Islamic World* announced a shift in practice:

> In future *Jumma* prayers will be celebrated at the Mosque every Friday afternoon at 2-30. There will be the usual meeting of members in addition every Friday evening at 8 o'clock.[83]

This announced addition of an afternoon Jumū'a allowed Quilliam, through Byrne, to claim in his 1896 Annual speech that, contrary to Asmay's allegation,

> Jumma and every other *Nimaz* in Liverpool is made exactly in the

---

82 *TC*, 08/11/1899, p.298.
83 *TC*, 11/09/1895, p.169.

same manner as it is in every Mosque of the Hanifee school of Muslims throughout the world.

In London, by then, Dollie's new mosque was holding full Islamic Friday prayers. Quilliam was officially aligning in practice with his close friend at the London Temporary Mosque. In practice, after a day's work, the converts in Brougham Terrace still preferred to gather on Friday evenings for plain discussion and entertainment, before performing the night prayer together at the mosque and heading for home.[84] Habits were hard to break. Nevertheless, by 1899, a regular Jumū'a Prayer was well established at the LMI. One reporter describes the event as follows:

> They say prayers at their Mosque in West Derby Road, and on a Friday— the Muslim prayer day—there is usually a very fair congregation. In addition to the ordinary members, there may be present a few Turks from the Turkish Consulate, and perhaps a handful of swarthy sailors from some Asian vessel then lying in the Mersey. Strangers [non-Muslims] are admitted to the service. It is a peculiar sight to see elderly Englishmen bowing towards Mecca, and repeating the well-known formula, the base of Islamism, '*La Il'ah illal'ah, Muhammed rasul Allah*'—'There is no God but God, and Muhammed is His Prophet'.[85]

From August 1900, *The Crescent* started to report Jumū'a prayers on a weekly basis, with the recurrent phrasing that "Jumma prayers were celebrated as usual on Friday last at the Liverpool mosque". A new term appeared in *The Crescent*, "khotba" (the Islamic sermon given by the imam), which was now given by Quilliam on a regular basis. It had previously only been used for the Eid al-Fitr speech given in Arabic by Barakatullah,[86] by visiting Ottoman intellectual Ubeydullah,[87] or by Quilliam himself for the Sultan's Jubilee.[88] A general shift in practice towards Islamic orthodoxy had emerged. The shift would be confirmed with the publication, for instance, of a primer on how to perform ablution, prayer, and even the *janāza* prayer

---

84 *TC*, 23/10/1895, p.267.
85 *TC*, idem. The strongest attack, however, during which the British muezzin was pelted from a street mob, occurred on a Sunday evening, after the Sunday service (*TC*, 09/01/1895, p.14).
86 *TC*, 05/06/1895, p.182.
87 *TC*, 18/03/1896, p.398
88 *TC*, 05/09/1900, p.146

for the deceased. By 1906, reports in *The Crescent* would run as follows:

> Jumma prayers were celebrated as usual at the Liverpool Mosque on Friday last, the 9th.... The Azan was given by Bro. Ahmed C. Brann, and the prayers were led and the Khutba recited by Bro. S. Mahmoud Bey.[89]

6. *The Ottoman Ban of Asmay's Book*

Quilliam had a private interview with Abdulhamid II on 2 May 1898 and reported that the caliph had told him that "the success of Islam in the British Isles lies very near to His Majesty's noble and generous heart." His second, successful trip to Istanbul was crowned by the caliph awarding him the Order of the Osmanieh (fourth class) ten days later, a prestigious honour normally given to civil servants and military personnel for services to the Ottoman state.[90] Twenty-nine days after Quilliam's private audience with the caliph, the Ministry of the Interior issued an order to the Ministry of Foreign Affairs to ban Asmay's *Islam in Liverpool* within the Ottoman domains, as it contained "harmful contents" (see entire text of the ban in Appendix 1). The plainest explanation is that Quilliam was able to appeal directly and successfully to the caliph for renewed recognition and support over the heads of any critics of the LMI. It might therefore be surmised that Quilliam asked for Asmay's book to be banned and that the caliph granted his request. That said, as the order does not give any detailed rationale, it should be noted that there were many reasons why the Ottomans might ban a book, for instance, any book imported from outside the Ottoman domains would have its contents examined and assessed.[91]

---

89 A.C. Brann, *Moslem Liturgical Prayer* (Liverpool: The Crescent Publishing Company, 1906); *TC*, 30/05/1906, p.345; 13/06/1906, pp.377, 379; 18/06/1906, p.393.

90 *TC*, 22/06/1898, p.391; Matt Sharp notes (pp.72–3) that Ottoman sources don't mention a private audience with the caliph but do confirm Quilliam's receipt of the Order of the Osman.

91 E. Boyar, "The Press and the Palace: The Two-Way Relationship between Abdulhamid II and the Press", *Bulletin of the School of Oriental and African Studies*, 69/3, 2006, pp.417–432; D.J. Cioeta, "Ottoman Censorship in Lebanon and Syria, 1876–1908", *International Journal of Middle East Studies*, 10/2, May 1979, pp.167–186; A. Polat, Subject to approval: Sanction and censure in Ottoman Istanbul, 1889–1923, PhD dissertation, University of Chicago, 2015, pp.87–94; I.K. Yosmaoğlu, "Chasing the Printed Word: Press Censorship in the Ottoman Empire, 1876–1913", *The Turkish Studies Association Journal*, 27/1–2, 2003, pp.15–49.

Two of Asmay's predictions were proven to be correct. Firstly, that Quilliam and the LMI would be able to recover from these criticisms, not least because of the propaganda power of *The Crescent* and *The Islamic World*. Secondly, despite some of the reforms that were enacted after 1895, Asmay foresaw that without a firm and orthodox foundation in transparency and accountability, the Institute would not survive Quilliam's departure. In 1908, this turned out to be true. When Quilliam departed from Liverpool for good, his son Billal closed the mosque and sold off Brougham Terrace. With no leadership or base, the LMI's convert community collapsed, never to recover.[92]

Today it is a common urge to look for historical heroes or founding figures who help to cultivate a sense of grounded identity for a faith community whose sense of belonging is often unfairly maligned and questioned. Looking to the past for clues as to how a universal Muslim faith might be meaningfully iterated in local culture and context is also an important part of this process. In this respect, the figure of Quilliam has loomed large in recent decades for converts and second- and third-generation British Muslims looking for routes towards and roots in this quest for harmonisation. This quest is often aspirational in tenor and, as such, can be prone to overlook history "warts and all". Yet if sometimes history does not always provide British Muslims, or Muslims in and of the West more generally, with ready-made models of past harmonization to learn from, the clarity they gain from a fuller understanding of their own past successes and failures in this regard will allow them to ponder questions of Muslim faith, identity, and belonging in the West with greater acuity and deeper self-understanding.

A Note on the Text and Appendixes

We have attempted a faithful translation while endeavouring to capture something of the original's literary flair and shifts in tone. We have retained key Ottoman Turkish terms in brackets with an emphasis upon religious terms, as there are times when Asmay deploys an Islamic or Turkish term to convey the meaning of what was a hybrid form of Anglo-Islam with

---

92 Geaves, *Islam in Victorian Britain*, pp.254–8; J. Gilham, *Loyal Enemies: British Converts to Islam*, 1850–1950 (London: Hurst, 2014), pp.117–121.

Nonconformist elements in its religious language and services. That there is discordance between the English terms used at the Liverpool Muslim Institute and Asmay's translation strategies is important to convey and preserve in the text.

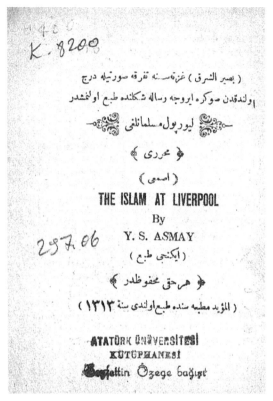

(بصير الشرق) غزة ته تفرقه صورتیله درج
اولندقدن صوکره ابروجه رساله شكلنده طبع اولنشدر
ليورپوله سلمانلنی

محرری

(اسمى)

THE ISLAM AT LIVERPOOL

By

Y. S. ASMAY

(ایکنجی طبع)

هر حق محفوظدر

(المؤيد مطبعه سنده طبع اولندى سنة ۱۳۱۳)

ATATÜRK ÜNİVERSİTESİ
KÜTÜPHANESİ
Seyfettin Özege bağışı

Picture 2: Title Page of Asmay's Islam in Liverpool (1896)

On occasion, Asmay inserts his own comments or glosses into the text in round brackets, which we have retained. This is especially true when he offers his own translations of Arabic or Persian texts in the text, as eagle-eyed readers will spot. Where needed, we have added our own glosses in square brackets for clarification of the text.

Where Asmay has reproduced English texts and then translated them, we have corrected these against the original source texts for mistakes, unless there has been a deliberate change of sense (evident in only one instance). We have omitted translations of the Ottoman Turkish rendering of the English texts in the original for obvious reasons but have noted any significant points about glosses made or translation strategies adopted.

We have retained Arabic and Persian texts where Asmay quoted them to preserve these primary sources – Barakatullah's two letters in Arabic and the transcription of the reception for Nasrullah Khan at the LMI in Persian – alongside our rendering of Asmay's own translations with his glosses in round brackets.

We have preserved Asmay's original subsection headers but have taken the liberty of naming the five unnamed sections as chapters with titles of our own devising.

Finally, we have marked the original pagination of the 112-page Ottoman Turkish text for ease of reference and citation, which are marked in bold and set in square brackets.

In Appendixes 1 and 2, we have included the other major primary source texts concerning the Keep–Asmay Crisis, namely the relevant Ottoman archival records in translation and edited extracts from the reports of the 1895 and 1896 reports in *The Crescent* of the LMI's annual general meetings. For any reader who wishes to consult with the full versions of these reports, back issues of *The Crescent* are archived online at the website of the Abdullah Quilliam Society based in the original building of the Liverpool Muslim Institute. In Appendix 3, we have provided detailed profiles of the main LMI members (besides Quilliam himself) who are mentioned in the text, much of it based on original archival research.

In general, throughout the whole book we have kept the verbatim spellings used in the original cited English sources, because the variant and oftentimes eccentric orthography records the development of English as an Islamic(ate) language.

If any mistakes or errors are found in the text, then please do contact us through Claritas Books, so they can be corrected in future editions of the book.

Acknowledgements

We would like to thank all those who fielded queries or helped us with this project such as Yakoob Ahmed, Cemil Aydin, Mehmet Emit, Ron Geaves, Samir Mahmoud, Umar Ryad, Matt Sharp, and members of the WhatsApp UK Muslim History Group. Special mention should be given to Muhammad Hasanov for drawing our attention to a surviving copy of Asmay's pamphlet at the University of Ankara, and to the relevant Ottoman archival documents; Arif Erbil for deciphering and translating the latter; Aburahman Abouhawas for transcribing the accounts of the Liverpool Muslim Institute meetings; Ramon Harvey for checking the translated Arabic excerpts; Roger Hull and Paul Keough of the Liverpool Public Records Office for assistance with archival research; Gökhan Göbel and Oruç Özel of TİYO for sending us background information on Asmay; Fozia Bora for providing critical feedback on the Introduction; and Wali-ur Rahman and Sheikh Sharif H. Banna for publishing this work through Claritas Books. Finally, thanks to our families for their continued support, care and understanding.

Any errors or mistakes are our own.

Y, R & M.
20 December 2020

YUSUF SAMIH ASMAY'S
ISLAM IN LIVERPOOL
(1896)

[1] After being published in instalments in *Basîr al-Sharq* newspaper, this is now printed as a pamphlet.

Islam in Liverpool
(ليورپول مسلمانلغي)

Yusuf Samih Asmay
(يوسف سميح اصمعي)

Second impression.
Printed at Al-Muayyad Printers in 1313AH. (Cairo) [2]

بسم الله الرحمن الرحيم

الحمد لله الذي أرسل رسوله بالهدى وزيّن الحق ليظهره على الدين كله وأمرنا باتباعه في كل ما جاء به و اوضحه في قوله و فعله صلى الله عليه وسلم وعلى آله وأصحابه الائمة الاعلام القائمين بعده بالتعاضد على تأييد كلمة الاسلام

In the name of God, Most Merciful, Most Compassionate.
All praise is due to God who sent His messenger with guidance and beautified the truth in order to make it manifest over all religion. We are commanded to follow him in everything that he came with and made clear in his word and deed, may God bless him and grant him peace. And [may God bless] his family and his companions who are leaders, and luminaries standing up after him to aid and support the word of Islam.

1
A FAINT SOUND CAME
FROM THE WEST

Eight years ago, a faint sound began to come from the West to the East. Realising that the sound was significant, the Muslim *umma* sat up and took notice, cupping their hands to their ears. Giving all their attention to the sound, they could only make out this sentence, "Islam has started to appear in England."

This sentence caught by the ear spread by word of mouth and as time went on more sentences were added to it. Exclusive pieces [3] and articles were written on it. Nonetheless, the matter was not fully understood.

Moreover, this sound, which should have lost its volume as it travelled further, instead grew stronger thanks to the continuous efforts of its provider and it gave joy to the ears of the faithful. Then more sentences came as follows:

An Englishman in the city of Liverpool located in Britain[93] is engaged with spreading the message of the graceful religion of Muhammad. The Muslim community has been growing bigger by the day there. An Islamic society (جمعیت اسلامیه) has been established. A mosque has been built. A mufti and imams have been appointed.

Was the news based on this story in reported speech tense enough to give us assurance of its veracity?[94]

As the days, weeks, months and years passed, one news article after another about our brothers-in-faith increasingly appeared.

---

93 Asmay literally uses an old Ottoman Turkish mumpsimus, "the island of England". It occurs several times in the original text, but it has been replaced by "Britain" throughout the translation.

94 The quote is in Turkish reported speech tense, which does not have a direct English equivalent.

Subsequently, publications by this community (جماعت) and association (جمعيه) arrived, which testified to how they conducted themselves. In Islamic countries (بلاد اسلاميه) in general and in the Ottoman dominions in particular, Muslim newspapers started to translate [4] and publish them with due attention.

From then onwards, all Islamic countries were aware that Islam had emerged in Liverpool. We started reading the contents of *The Crescent* – meaning *Al-Hilâl* – a weekly newspaper, the most important and acclaimed publication of the Liverpool Muslim Institute, translated every week in our newspapers.

Therefore, no one harboured any doubts that this news was unsound, unverified or untrustworthy. Everyone learned the name of Mr. Abdullah Quilliam, the founder and the head of the Liverpool Muslim Institute and its community, [but] news of reservations from certain persons who deserve to be called precautious rather than nit-pickers has [also] been heard.

So, who is Abdullah Quilliam? Why did he embrace Islam by leaving behind the Protestantism into which he was born and raised? What kind of resources has he relied upon to spread the religion of Muhammed among the English, who are infamous for their bigotry? Is he blessed with [learning of] anything from the Islamic sciences? And so forth, etc.

At first glance, doesn't addressing these queries seem reasonable? [5] Well, changing one's religion is clearly not like changing one's shirt.

It is worth considering that for a man, who would not even like to change his shirt unless its collar gets dirty, leaving the religion that he was born into and was brought up in and embracing another one requires much study and research on religions generally so that his conscience is satisfied in all respects. First of all, a person who sets out sincerely to change his religion becomes convinced of its fundamental shortcomings after examining it. Then he researches other religions in great detail and selects one from among them that he sees as the true one. Otherwise, [without this comparative approach,] it should be concluded that this person is not serious at all.

It is akin to attention-seeking people putting themselves into all kinds of situations just to gain fame or inconstant lovesick youth changing from one season to the next.

When Mr. Abdullah Quilliam visited the Abode of Felicity,[95] the seat of the Islamic caliphate, we read about it in our papers. [6]

---

95 Quilliam first visited Constantinople (Istanbul) in 1891.

Almost every day, we would see under Abdullah Quilliam Efendi's name the translation [from English] of his life, how and why he found guidance [i.e., converted to Islam],[96] and the achievements of the Islamic Institute that he established in Liverpool. In brief, we learnt everything about him.

During those days the papers in Istanbul would even report how the crowd carried him over their heads from the court entrance to his office[97] when this man of many virtues, who happened to be an attorney in Liverpool, won a case thanks to his proficiency in law, his competency in rhetoric and clarity of speech.

The Muslim community's experience with Europe, which has equally developed in every aspect, and with England in particular, has made them apprehensive as their tongues were swollen from the dainties that they took from them thinking they were sweet. Hence, they would not give up wondering "Why has Mr. Quilliam become Muslim? Could it be due to a commercial interest?"

One could even find sceptics who thought that he considered the name of Islam as some sort of capital that would bring him profit in the form of charity, donations, financial assistance and grants from the Islamic countries.

Back then this unworthy author used to think as much too: considering that there are no people in the world as attention-seeking as Englishmen [7] and they would go to great lengths just to make their name appear in the papers just once, even to the point of sacrificing their lives to this end while suffering all sorts of privations, might not our friend Mr. Quilliam be excused for doing the same [in the cause of promoting Islam]?

Be that as it may, some friends remonstrated with me for not going to Liverpool to ascertain the truth with my own eyes by visiting my new brothers-in-Islam and their mosque, even though I had previously travelled from Egypt to England twice and visited London and its surrounding cities.[98] They were right to reprimand me, as it would be highly appreciated if I could bring them news about the Liverpool Muslim Institute and its

---

96 Throughout the original text, Asmay added his own glosses in round brackets, which have been retained in the translation in the same format.

97 W.H. Quilliam, "Islam in England", *Religious Review of Reviews*, 1/3 (1891), pp.159–65 for mention of Quilliam and the acquitted being carried on the shoulders of the crowd after a murder case at the Chester Assizes (pp.164–5).

98 Asmay visited England three times between 1891 and 1895. An account of his first journey was published in instalments under the name, *Seyâhat-ı Asmay* (*Asmay's Travels*).

Muslim culture (مسلمانلغي), instead of talking through my hat about the foggy English weather and the values and customs of its natives.

I had my excuses for not having made it to Liverpool before. Nonetheless, I had heard the following from some Ottomans that I came across in London:

> Yes! It has a little rhyme but no reason. Their Muslim practices (مسلمانلغي) are not like ours. They have recast the Noble Qur'an as Psalms and put it to music. They perform prayers (نماز) with music playing. [8]

My curiosity grew even more with this news and I, taking it upon myself as a duty, promised myself that if I were to go to England again I would definitely visit Liverpool in order to meet my new brothers-in-faith and study them in every respect. Thank God I have succeeded. For exactly thirty-three days starting from the 23rd of this past month of Muharram [16 July 1895] I have stayed in Liverpool and attended the mosque three times a week and met with one of our new brothers-in-faith every day to interview them. Apart from that I have also gathered information from an Ottoman intellectual,[99] who has been staying there since the 18th [11 July], and from some local Christians with whom contact has been established. I have noted everything in my journal daily to make sure I did not forget anything. In addition to that, I am obliged to tell my dear readers that I informed Mr. Abdullah Quilliam I was going to publish a pamphlet entitled *Islam in Liverpool* (ليورپول مسلمانلغي) upon my return to Egypt and that I was going to be frank about whatever I had seen and heard, provided that I had verified and heard from them [the Liverpool Muslims] directly, with complete freedom and without concealing anything or obscuring the truth and [ascertaining] the real situation. [He replied:]

> By all means, please do write as such. We would be pleased with that. You are entirely free to compose your piece as you see fit, [9] while giving your own perspective on our character and customs.

I have seen and noted in the contents of this pamphlet my impressions that can never quite capture the immediacy of seeing it for oneself. Therefore, may the readers forgive my shortcomings as a writer if they find that some of it does not correspond to what they have previously heard.

---

99 Not identified.

2
THE BRITISH CHARACTER

I am obliged to proceed with this second section before going on to examine the Liverpool Muslims directly, which is the main goal of this pamphlet, in order to give my dear readers a general impression of England. As a matter of fact, not every aspect of England can be compared to those of other civilized countries, for their lifestyle, civilization, character and customs are all particular to themselves. Although they are next-door neighbours to the French, whose every trait is very well-known to us thanks to their (widely spoken) language, the civilization and [10] moral character of these two nations are contrary to each other.

The People
In the island we call England or Britain live people with three different languages. The first among them are the English, who are the dominant group; the official language is English, and the official religion is Protestantism.[100] The second and the third peoples are the Scots and the Welsh. Although they have their own languages and books and newspapers written in the Latin alphabet, their language is in the vernacular and in public they are expected to speak in English. The Scots language has the consonant "ç" like Turkish and Italian and is not as exhausting to listen to or as difficult to pronounce as Welsh.

The Welsh language is unpleasant to the ear. Its vocabulary is full of words with the letter "خ" and it is pronounced from the nasal passage. It

---

100 Namely, the established Anglican Protestantism of the Church of England and the established Anglican Church of Wales (until the latter was disestablished in 1920). The Presbyterian Church of Scotland, or the Kirk, was granted formal autonomy over spiritual affairs in 1921. In general, Asmay is either ignorant of or disinclined to differentiate between the various Protestant sects to simplify his account for his intended audience.

even has a peculiar letter. A Welshman, whom I met on the day I visited the town of Beaumaris in Wales on this trip, wrote down a word made of fifty-six letters in my journal as a souvenir.

Although the English, the Scots and the Welsh are fond of their country, government and laws, they do not refrain from disliking or insulting one other, such as saying that the other is [11] unfriendly, selfish or thick-headed.

I humbly submit that generally looking down on one another is a common malady among people of different linguistic groups. Thus, the people of Britain are hardly exceptional in that regard.

Social Rank and Moral Character

Every nation divides its community into three segments – the educated, the middle class and the commoners. Even we [Ottomans] have groups ranked as head, body and tail.[101] This classification is, however, unwarranted in the English case.

Although some authors have written that there are ten different classes, namely kings, courtiers, senior clergy, landed gentry, scholars, officers, tradespeople, craftspeople, farmers, and labourers, and that each has different customs and virtues, it is not true.

Based on my knowledge of social mores, I can declare that English society cannot be subjected to any other formula but this: there are two groups of people, namely, the wealthy, meaning the educated and cultivated, and the other group is the commoners. In England, nobility, leadership, scholarship, favour, [and] rank – in brief, all qualities that would place someone in a privileged position – are in the hands of the wealthy. [12]

In England, if a man is rich, even if his lineage goes back to a teapot, everything will serve his person. Nonetheless, one has to admit that this first group of above-mentioned people avoid commenting on their government's foreign policy, based on the delicate point that they [who enact it] are true to their word, the right men for the job, trustworthy in their personal relationships, sober in demeanour, coolheaded, taciturn, [and] thoughtful.

Some people keen on statistics have written that this part of the population does not exceed 60,000. From the Divine decree, this handful of people possess the power, own land and property – houses and mansions

---

101 Literally, "lowlife".

and shops – in short, all the present and future wealth of Britain, while leaving the millions of people who make up the second class out on the street. It looks as if the "common people", as they are dubbed, can only rely on their physical strength to earn enough to put food on the table, while the upper classes remain rich and contented, as this [gross inequality] is at their specific [behest] and [reveals] the true spirit of England.

Thus, those at the bottom [13] never even harbour hopes of getting rich and being among the upper classes.[102]

[So,] the head will stay on top and the tail will remain at the bottom. Lords sire lords, and the poor give birth to the poor: they starve, die and are buried without a shroud.[103]

In brief, ranking classes in the population is like the organs of the body. Hence the head is always the head even if it is just a cabbage[104] and makes the foot suffer many hardships and destroys the body to the point of extinction. On the other hand, the poor foot will remain a foot even if it surmounts the castle and saves the body's life in the nick of time by bearing its heavy weight.

Moreover, I would like to observe that the upper classes are strangers to the lower classes. The rich feel repulsed by the faces of the poor, let alone being acquainted, having a connection, or [even] relations with one another.

They are not entirely wrong [to feel repulsed by the poor] though, but it is unnecessary to dwell on this matter here. In our society, the wealthy landowner and the peasant, the poor and the rich are not all that different from each other in terms of moral character, custom, honesty or generosity. So, our notables deign to eat from a communal plate with our shepherds. [14] Then one heads to his orchards through the riverbed while the other heads to the mountains for his flock. And they would not be reproached or scorned by anyone for having behaved that way.

The case is the total opposite in England. It is strange that while the upper classes mostly have good manners the lower classes are so vulgar.

---

102 When describing the class structure in England the author alternately uses خواص (khawāṣ) and عوام ('awām) from Arabic, or head and foot from Turkish, because there is no direct equivalent due to lack of a similar structure other than the expression of "those at the head" (of the country) and those at the foot, meaning those at the bottom, or the masses.

103 In Islamic custom, the deceased is normally shrouded out of respect; in other words, they are buried in a pauper's grave due to lack of means.

104 Literally, "gourd".

Although many centuries have passed since the dawn of their civilization, they display a degree of barbarity that could not even be found among savages. Filthiness, treachery, ingratitude, callousness, drunkenness, indifference to religion, ignorance, [and] idiocy abound among the commoners and the poor of England. The English elite, who, while protective of animals, have not found sensible solutions to offer protection to the young and desolate girls who have run away from the abuses of common men and end up falling into all sorts of trouble.

One is astonished by the police reports and news of divorce that are published in the daily papers. Who would believe that when the common people get angry, they can beat their women to the point of death? Who would believe that the police jail thousands of poor girls, who get drunk and make trouble whilst on holiday? [15]

Vulgarity is observable in every act of the common people in England. The way they laugh, the way they sing, spitting frequently in random places, their remarks, faces, selves and expressions are rough and coarse.

Also, they are very filthy to such a degree that if a man of refinement happened to walk through their neighbourhoods, he would feel like vomiting for hours, wouldn't he? Yes, he would.

Selling off his wife for a glass of beer or a shot of gin, sleeping with his daughters, cutting his child, a mother's beloved, with razors, coercing a husband to poison his wife, a child killing his parents, and other such depraved acts seem like taxes for the common people in England.[105]

They guffaw so ribaldly that one might think a turkey is gobbling. Those who smoke a black and a very bad tobacco using a short pipe cover the ground around them with phlegm. Their drinking habits are so bad that the police constables designate specific carriages for the drunk.

Unlike the rest of Europe, all shops and businesses are shut down on Sundays in England and it turns into [16] a place of mourning thanks to the influence of the priests, but these poor clergymen are unable to do the same for the pubs. There are as many people attending the church as there are going to the pub. While women of the Protestant elite, who are known for their religious zeal, go to the church three times on Sundays, the common people's degree of indifference to religion is beyond words. Common men who would not go to church to worship God or even leave

---

105 Asmay has no compunction in presenting the most extreme behaviours heard in court and reported in the popular press as representative of the general social norms of the English masses.

a penny on the priest's charity plate will go to a pub instead and waste their money on whisky, beer and gin. The only reason I could ascertain for this behaviour was their ignorance and idiocy. But they are prevented from acquiring knowledge and virtues through attending school for years due to their poverty and [lack of] basic needs.

Marriage

As will become apparent in the coming pages, the subject of marriage has relevance to this pamphlet. Therefore, I had to write about it. It should not be regarded as superfluous. If we are to ask if marriage is difficult in England or if it is easy, we should note to which gender the question is posed because the answer will vary accordingly. What applies to one gender will not apply to the other. **[17]**

If you pose this question to an Englishman, he will say there is nothing easier than finding a pretty girl with good manners to marry. Admiring a girl, wooing her and getting married is as easy as drinking a glass of water and as quick as purchasing a pair of gloves at a reasonably priced shop. Time is money, isn't it?

Now address the same question to the fairer sex and see what answer you get. After thinking for a while and sighing deeply she will tell you there is nothing in this land as difficult as finding a suitable husband. In a country where nothing other than money and beauty are prized, finding a husband would of course be difficult. Let me explain what might be concluded from two different answers to the same question and what is the animating force behind it: the majority of the people who travel to the colonies for employment as officers for trade or to earn a living are men, while those who remain must endure hardship in order to make a living. Particularly due to frequent coupling there are no less than half-a-dozen girls in every household. Due to the scarcity of husbands in the country, getting married is an easy task for a man but a difficult one for a woman.[106]

---

106 There is evidence for the first part of this claim. According to the Cambridge Group for the History of Population and Social Structure, in England and Wales there were 92 men aged 14–64 for every hundred women in the same age range for each of the decennial censuses between 1851–1911. Some 22.6 million migrated from the British Isles between 1815–1914; and there was a concerted effort after 1850 to "find colonial outlets for Britain's surplus female population", see M. Harper, "British Migration and the Peopling of the Empire" in A. Porter and A. Low (eds) *The Oxford History of the British Empire: The Nineteenth Century*, Vol. 3 (Oxford: University Press, 1999), pp.75–87 (quote on p.81).

Girls [18] seeking husbands advertise dowries worth thousands of pounds in various marriage magazines but they cannot easily achieve their goals. So long as a girl finds a husband she wants, it does not matter if he is in Canada or New Zealand. She immediately leaves her homeland, and even abandons her church, and travels to Calcutta or the Cape of Good Hope.

In this regard, through our brother Mr. Quilliam, a few girls have found guidance [converted to Islam] and travelled to India after marrying Indians. The ladies said that they would even wear a hay-sack let alone a veil if it was their husbands' wish. I also heard when I was there that a Turk from the Black Sea coast who, working as a sailor on the ships, married a girl in this manner and took her back to his hometown.

Freedom of Religion

In Britain, there is truly freedom of religion. The government, which guarantees the safeguarding of public security, never prevents people of different religions from building their places of worship, promoting their faith or performing their rituals, and regards protecting them in every aspect, [such as] respecting their community [or] keeping them safe from any aggression as a duty.

If something does not harm others nor [19] violates public security, it will be safe from government intervention and, if the situation calls for it, it will be given protection. In brief, religion is as free as trade in England

The lack of [formal] relations between the Catholic and Protestant Churches has not prevented them from building their churches opposite or next to one other. Both communities go to their places of worship peacefully and conduct their worship in absolute safety.[107]

In England, even Judaism is treated the same way. Jews have their synagogues and conduct their worship on Saturdays. From neither the government nor any rowdy types among the Christian population do they see any aggression or harm. Catholics marry Protestant girls and Protestants marry Catholic girls; they get married and change their church.

Even Jews marry [with other communities]. Many Orthodox Greeks get married in England. They even marry Muslims. A few of the Turks

---

107 The author betrays a lack of insight into the history of the conflictual relationship between Catholics and Protestants in the Victorian Age, that was ongoing, albeit less openly violent, at the time of his visits to England, see E.R. Norman, *Anti-Catholicism in Victorian England* (London: Routledge, 1968).

I know have English wives. I have heard that there are also English girls who marry Indian Zoroastrians and go to India.

Protestantism is the official religion in England, but, [20] although its followers seem quite conservative, their religious zeal does not exceed its boundaries. [Therefore,] nobody stands in the way of those who would like to promote their religion.

As mentioned above, so long as they do not violate public safety and order, all activities and things are free and safe from government intervention. Even nihilist, socialist and anarchist societies of mischief address the crowds in parks and squares and policemen attend their events just like other members of the public. When asked why they do not stop them, they reply, "This is a free country."

In England, you are also free to be a Muslim. In a town close to London called Woking, there is a mosque built by an Indian. The Jewish family that resides nearby and takes care of the mosque says that they have never witnessed aggression from anyone and there has been no vile or wicked action toward the Muslim community who gather there for Eid or Friday prayers.[108] After all, no one has time to engage with such useless things in England. Everybody [21] is at work.

Even the unemployed or those sacked factory workers gather at factory forecourts to lobby the owners to find a way to make a few pennies.

Why would they gather at the doors of the places of worship where there is no hope of getting bread? The strict police regulations also prevent any kind of aggression against other religions that would come out of popular bigotry. Is there still such bigotry among the common people in England as there is in Europe generally?

In England, were it not for social convention, they would not even listen to the melodious voices of those reciting the Honourable Testament in tune[109] with the organ for an hour-and-a-half every Sunday at their places of worship.

The Liverpool Muslim Institute has so far suffered no aggression or assault.

---

108 Asmay is referring to Gottlieb Wilhelm Leitner (1840–99), who while born a Hungarian Jew had converted to Jewish Christianity. A polyglot and renowned educationist, he was instrumental in establishing the University of the Punjab and later the Oriental Institute in Woking, and built the first purpose-built mosque in Britain in 1889 that was partly financed by the Begum of Bhopal.

109 The author is referring here to the singing of hymns.

On a Sunday at 7pm when Mr. Arthur Hasan Radford,[110] the muezzin of the Liverpool Mosque, who, I heard from our brother Mr. Quilliam, works as a marine boiler riveter for a living, was making the call to prayer (reciting the *adhān*) as usual in Arabic and English [22] at the first floor window of the house dedicated to the mosque, they yelled at him saying, "Why the hell are you shouting man?!" and threw stones at him. His right-hand wrist was injured.[111] They tell this incident to all the brothers-in-Islam who come from the East and visit the Liverpool mosque as they did to my unworthy self. They did not tell me about any other offensive incident, nor did I hear of another from anyone else.[112]

Sectarian Strife

In England, there are various sects that broke away from Protestantism, the most famous of which are the Quakers that was established by a madman named George Fox in 1642,[113] and the Unitarian Churches.

For the Quakers, christening and similar Christian rituals that are normally considered mandatory are forbidden and their churches are very simple. They do not have priests and do not recite the Honourable Bible during their worship.

For those who would like to learn more about this subject, *Kashf al-mukhab-bā ʿan funūn Ūrūpā* by Ahmed Faris Efendi is recommended.[114] [23]

---

110 See Appendix 3 for Radford's biography.

111 This attack took place on Sunday, 6 January 1895. According to *The Crescent*: "The snow lay heavily on the ground, and when the Muezzin, Bro. A. Hassan Radford, went to give the Azan a mob of Christians who had collected near the Mosque rushed forward and pelted the 'caller to prayer' with snowballs. He was struck on various parts of the body, and one of his hands was severely cut open by the sharp edge of a stone which had been enclosed in one of the snowballs. Some hundreds of missiles were thrown, and many of them contained stones." (09/01/1895, p.15) When arrested and charged, one of the assailants, a local apprentice baker, explained that he "joined the fun" and that he had acted as a devout Protestant: "They are heathens, and they don't worship God." (*TC*, 23/01/1895, p.27)

112 For a detailed account of anti-Muslim rejection of the LMI and its members: B.D. Singleton, "'Heave Half a Brick at Him': Hate Crimes and Discrimination against Muslim Converts in Late Victorian Liverpool", *Journal of Muslim Minority Affairs*, 37/1, 2017, pp.1–13, DOI: 10.1080/13602004.2017.1294376. Asmay was ill-informed about the numerous attacks against worshippers at the LMI. According to Quilliam, on different occasions, windows were broken, members pelted with mud and even lighted fireworks were thrown into the mosque during prayer. (*TC*, 23/01/1895, p.27)

113 The usual year given for the establishment of Fox's Society of Friends is 1652.

114 Aḥmad Fāris Al-Shidyāq (1804–87), *Unveiling the Arts of Europe* (Tunis,

The Unitarian Church is the *muwaḥḥidīn* group of Christianity. They are convinced that Allah is One and say that the Christian statement about our Prophet Lord Jesus (حـضرت عيـسى ع م افندمـز) being the son of Allah (ابـن اللہ) should be regarded as an expression of respect and homage to him.

When I was in Brighton [in 1891], I came across a few of them and tried to learn something about the creed of their faith (اعتقـاد), which I shall abstain from writing about now as this subject has no relevance to our pamphlet.

Let's cut to the chase. I can observe that England deserves its reputation as a land of tedious ambition. One day in London when I was crossing the street with a respectable and gracious English friend of mine, I noticed a flag that I have never seen before at one of the first floor windows of a house and asked my friend which country it belonged to.

My dear friend, this flag belongs not to a government of this world but to one of the spiritual domains. We have the flags of all sorts of ecumenical organisations[115] here. In England, just as there are multiple railroads to reach a city there are multiple ways to reach heaven. Although the English are free to choose any of the roads to heaven, [24] they prefer to remain Protestant to achieve happiness; in other words, to get a high position and rank in life and to attain the heavens of the angels in death.

1238AH/1867).

115 Asmay is noting the diversity of voluntary societies and agencies that flourished in Victorian cities: temperance societies, societies for the distribution of religious literature, for defence of Protestantism, of dissenter's rights, for opposition to Anglo- and Roman Catholicism, etc. These societies and agencies reflected the vitality and diversity of Victorian religious life and for Asmay were a powerful demonstration of religious freedom of expression in England.

3
RELIGIOUS LIFE AT THE
LIVERPOOL MUSLIM INSTITUTE

The verdict is clear. As you will see in the following pages, there are criticisms that will be put forward regarding the Liverpool Muslim community and Mr. Quilliam, who is, in short, their head. I am unsure if I need to remind [the reader] that this criticism has nothing to do with their religious creed (عقيـده).

There is no license to doubt the faith (ايمان) and Islam of the members of the Liverpool Muslim Institute. It is obviously meaningless to say this or that about persons, who have borne witness that Allah is One without equal and Muhammed is His true messenger and have accepted and affirmed the six fundamental articles of faith in Islam.[116]

However, although it [the Liverpool Muslim Institute] stands on the same fundamentals, [25] the structure that they have built does not resemble ours in certain regards. The reason for this is that Mr. Quilliam has set out to do it as he thought most fitting and in accordance with his own customs, but without consulting Islamic scholars or literature. This can be reproached so long as the criticism offered does not overstep the mark. As he is the founder and president [of the Liverpool Muslim Institute], he has the primary responsibility for the rightness and direction of what he has established.

The President

The Islamic leader of Liverpool is the attorney Mr. William Henry Quilliam, whose office is at 18 Manchester Street in the city. He is known among the Muslims (بـين الاسـلام) as Sheikh Abdullah Quilliam Efendi. Mr. William Henry Quilliam is his official name as he is not known or recognized as Sheikh Abdullah by his government or his

---

116 Literally, "I believe in God, His angels, His books, His prophets, the Day of Judgement and Predestination, for good or ill."

fellow Englishmen (جماعـة).

Had Mr. Quilliam known that changing one's name is not one of the conditions of becoming a Muslim (شروط اسـلام) but only indicates one's origin, would he still find it necessary to give his name as Abdullah, which he does not officially carry, amongst the people of Islam?

He is a good-humoured, cheerful Englishman of medium height and a slim build, with a ginger beard and intelligent eyes. He is a talented public speaker and is well-versed in legal casuistry, it is said. Although I do not know his exact age, he seems to be between forty and forty-five.[117]

[26] In his legal practice, he is famous for winning separation and divorce cases. Among his people, he ranks among the commoners.

The reason for his guidance [to Islam] was his meeting with the people of Islam (اهـل اسـلام) during a visit to Morocco on a holiday (this word coming from "holy day"). In Tangiers and a few other Moroccan cities – through a translator, I presume – he met and got to know many Muslims, admiring their Islamic moral character (اخـلاق اسـلامیه). Upon his return home, he carefully studied the English translation of the Noble Qur'an and Islamic books in English after which he became convinced that Islam was the true religion. Thereupon he accepted Islam and announced that he was a Muslim. This is how he narrates it.[118]

Although for two years following his acceptance of Islam, he could not make any English [person] Muslim, he did not become defeatist and give up promoting the message of Islam.

His mother, Mrs. [Harriet] Holehouse Quilliam, accepted Islam and took the name of Mrs. Khadija Holehouse Quilliam, thus becoming the first Khadija among the Liverpool Muslims. After that her husband,

---

117 W.H. Quilliam was thirty-nine at the time of Asmay's visit.

118 Quilliam's first published work on Islam, "The Mysteries of Moslem Theology", *The Kneph*, November 1885, 58–60, shows that he relied heavily upon George Sale's translation of the *Koran*, Washington Irving's *Life of Mahomet*, and John Reynell Morell's *Turkey: Past and Present*. He also recommended a list of selected other Orientalist works and travelogues, including the works of the comparative religionist, Max Muller. For an analysis and reproduction of this article, see A. Abouhawas, "'The Mysteries of Moslem Theology': Abdullah Quilliam's First Published Work on Islam from 1885", *EveryDay Muslim*, 20 April 2020, https://www.everydaymuslim.org/blog/the-mysteries-of-moslem-theology-sheikh-abdullah-quilliams-first-published-writing-on-islam-from-1885/, accessed 14 July 2019; see also "Islam in England", *The Star*, 16 December 1890, p.4. Quilliam privately converted in 1886 after his period of self-study and publicly announced his Islam and began preaching it in 1887, see Monro, p.31.

Mr. Quilliam's [step-]father, **[27]** Mr. Holehouse, became Muslim.[119] Subsequently he started to have success in his religious efforts [of calling to Islam].

Mr. Quilliam has two wives. The first of them[120] has not accepted Islam and it is said she insists that she wants to die in the Protestant tradition she was born and brought up in. He has four children by this woman. He met his second wife[121] before getting married to her (قبل العقد). After her acceptance of Islam, they got married according to Muslim rites. As the second wife is not recognized legally by the Liverpool authorities, when death (امر الله) seizes Mr. Quilliam it is said this poor woman and her children will not officially inherit anything from him. He has four children by her too.[122] More detail on this matter will come later.

Mr. Quilliam keeps his wives in two separate houses.[123]

The Muslim Institute

The Muslim Institute, of which we heard news of its existence in Liverpool, does not have a charter or regulations, elected committee members, a fixed day for meetings, written procedures for analysing or making decisions regarding its income and expenses, a treasurer, or a secretary as such. Whenever Mr. Quilliam feels like it and is available, he gathers those from among the converts (مهتدي) that suit his purpose and he informs them about his ideas, his thinking, or even his decisions **[28]** by having a chat with them so that he would be entitled to write exaggeratedly that he had conducted a Muslim Institute meeting, that speeches were delivered, and that decisions were taken in the next issue of *The Crescent* newspaper.

When this unworthy author was there, through a similar gathering they discussed the expulsion of Mrs. Nafeesa Keep from the Institute and sending her back to America. This poor woman came to Liverpool after resigning from her role as a secretary with Mr. Muhammed Webb,

---

119 See Appendix 3 for their biographical details.

120 Hannah Johnston, who married Quilliam at the Fairfield Wesleyan Chapel in 1879, see Appendix 3 for her biographical details.

121 Mary Lyon, whom Quilliam officially married at the Preston Registry Office in 1910 after Hannah's death from cancer in 1909. See Mary's biographical details in Appendix 3.

122 Quilliam's fifth child by Mary Lyon, May Habeebah, was born in 1897.

123 See Appendix 3 for details on Mary Lyon and her living arrangements with Quilliam and his wife Hannah.

whom we heard is spreading the religion [of Islam] (نـشر ديـن) in America.[124] It is said that she became a writer and dispatcher at Mr. Quilliam's printing press for a salary of only £2. The meeting was held because she was accused of saying inappropriate things about the converts, especially the young ones, of denigrating the [Liverpool] Muslim community to Muslims coming from the East to visit the mosque, and of writing letters against Quilliam and Maulana Barakatullah to His Highness Nasrullah Khan, the Crown Prince of Afghanistan, who was in London at the time. The members **[29]** refused the poor woman's pleas to be sent to a Muslim country instead of being exiled back to America. One day when I had the opportunity to ask Barakatullah the reason [for this refusal], he replied, "If she goes to Islamic countries, it will not be good for us because she will keep badmouthing us to every Muslim she comes across." They are right [to think that way].

Mrs. Nefeesa Keep is an American woman, who knows German and French, can write very eloquent articles in English, and is good at typewriting. She has infuriated the Muslim community, and particularly Quilliam, because she was a fifty-five-year-old woman[125] in need and was keen to meet with Muslims visiting from the East and tried her best in the tasks she was given.

The Liverpool Muslim Institute is a fictitious body. In reality, it consists [only] of our brother Mr. Quilliam. Liverpool, and especially Manchester, which is forty minutes from Liverpool by train, never fails to have a community of distinguished Muslims who, coming from India and other Islamic countries for trade,[126] have taken residency. Moreover,

---

124 See Introduction and Appendix 3 for biographical details on Nafeesa Keep and her dispute with Quilliam and the Liverpool Muslim Institute. For more on Alexander Russell Webb, see U.F. Abd-Allah, *A Muslim in Victorian America* (New York: Oxford University Press, 2006); P.D. Bowen, *A History of Conversion to Islam, Volume 1: White American Muslims before 1975* (Leiden: Brill, 2015), Chs 3 and 5; Sharp, Ch. 3; B.D. Singleton (ed.), *Yankee Muslim* (Rockwell, MD: Wildside Press, 2006).

125 M.T. Nafeesa Keep was fifty-one in 1895.

126 By 1895, Muslim traders in Manchester were mainly Moroccan and Syrian. A group of around forty cotton textile merchants and clerks, led by Ottoman Consul Mustapha Karsa, frequently visited the LMI for religious events, some of which indicated strong allegiance to the Sultan and to the central Ottoman authority. Some of these Syrian traders, such as the Mokaiesh or the Asha families, are listed by Asmay below as having attended Amir Nasrallah Khan's visit to the LMI. The Moroccan textile traders, who were not Ottoman subjects, had less interest in the LMI.

there is the Liverpool Ottoman Consul,[127] who can be considered a representative of the caliphal seat. Shouldn't it have been most necessary to appoint the Consuls as permanent committee members in such an Islamic society? So long as **[30]** Mr. Quilliam is President of the Institute, they should have been part of it.

The Muslim Institute should have established with a [legally-binding] charter to govern the recording and designation of donations, which do not fail to arrive from Muslim countries, as Islamic endowments (اوقاف اسلاميه) do, to be used to help the impoverished converts with money, to educate the Muslim children for free and to publish religious books.

The Muslim Institute should have allocated a certain amount from its donated income for our brother Mr. Quilliam's use as president and published its annual, itemised, charitable expenditure in *The Crescent* newspaper.

I guess it would be unsubstantiated to claim that [a genuine] Islamic association in Liverpool exists as none of this has happened. The received donations were neither published in *The Crescent* nor have any rules or regulations been instituted.

The Muslim Community

When I was visiting the house that is designated as a mosque, I asked the venerable Mr. Quilliam the following, "How many men and women have you been an instrumental part in their accepting Islam over the past eight years?" [He replied:] **[31]**

Although I can't recall exactly, it is about 200. I have a logbook where I keep all their names. But now it is with His Highness Nasrullah Khan, who is in London at the moment. I will tell you when I bring it back.

However, the total number of names on the list that I have managed to get through the American Mrs. Nafeesa Keep, to whom I have mentioned this, is somehow far less [than 200].

The abovementioned list that was prepared by Mr. Quilliam and presented to His Highness Nasrullah Khan, the Crown Prince of Afghanistan, included the names of male and female converts, but also the names of others.

---

127 The Ottoman Consul-Generals for Liverpool were Esad Kenan Bey and then Tahsin Bey from August 1895.

The total on the list is no more than seventy-five, out of which forty-two are women and girls. It will be provided in due course.

The Printing Press

Three ground-floor rooms that open on to one another in a house at 32 Elizabeth Street in Liverpool accommodates Quilliam's printing press where *The Crescent* and other works published in the name of the Liverpool Muslim Institute are printed. [32]

The monthly paper called *The Islamic World* is also printed here.

This printing house is Mr. Quilliam's property and not that of the fictitious Liverpool Muslim Institute or the charity as has been advertised.

The newspapers printed here serve as the [Institute's] means of communication with the Muslim persons and countries that Quilliam sends them to. That the proceeds of sales go to Muslim charity as is presumed or advertised is foolish chatter. As mentioned, the printing press consists of three sections, the first of which is the manager's room, the second is the typesetter's room, and the third is the printing press.

In the whole world, according to Mr. Quilliam, it is only the publications of this printing press that will gather the ideas of Turks, Arabs, Persians, Indians, Afghans and other nations of Islam in one place thus making them one family. By its newspapers promoting the idea of Islamic unity (إتحاد اسلام) all Muslims will be gathered under Quilliam's banner, so that [33] they will politically prevail over other nations.

When I stated the truth and averred that the language of Muslims is not English, but that knowledge is with our Prophet, the Imam of Muslims. Muslims are brothers and sisters and while they are spiritually connected, they are physically connected too through the call of "O Muslims" by the caliph of the prophet of the Lord of the Worlds. If you publish *The Crescent* in Arabic and choose the seat of the caliphate as the disseminating point for your publications, it would be regarded as authoritative among the Muslims. [To all this,] the respectable person did not confirm or deny. Also, according to some, the printing press is his means of business.

Mosque

It consists of a single house located at 8 Brougham Terrace, West Derby Road. The house's facade has a door and a window. It has three storeys.

Generally, houses [in England] are not larger than this as they do not have the custom of two families living together.

There is a sign in white paint hanging on the door of this house that reads as follows: [34]

THERE IS ONLY ONE GOD AND
MOHAMED IS HIS PROPHET
LIVERPOOL MOSQUE
MOSLEM INSTITUTE
PUBLIC LECTURES EVERY SUNDAY
EVENING AT 7 O'CLOCK[128]
[...]

A tall, [35] elderly, local man[129] with a white beard and a white hand-kerchief around his neck, who lives on the second floor of the house as the doorman or caretaker, stands at the door. When you step inside after greeting him you find yourself in a long and narrow corridor. After reading the "For Members Only" sign on the door of the first room on your left, you walk inside and find a piano standing on the left with a lot of music scores and 8-10 old fezzes in various colours, with a Persian fur

---

128 By the time of Asmay's visit, the external noticeboard had undergone changes. Clark (1891) and Pool (1892) both note use of the terms "Church of Islam" and "Divine Service". Clark remarks upon a more discreet notice over the fireplace in the front parlour, informing the Muslim visitors that, along with the services on Sundays (here called "Sunday services"), there are also "Divine Services every Friday at 9 o'clock". In 1893, a new notice board is placed on the outer wall of the building, with "the addition of the emblem of Islam, the Crescent and Star" (*TC*, 04/03/93, pp.51–2). This 1893 sign, which is the one Asmay describes here, has lost the two syncretic terms of "Church" and "service", and the Sunday events are now presented as "Public lectures". Kelly's Directory (1894) continues, however, to list the LMI as the "Church of Islam Mosque". These shifts in terminology testify to the difficulties met by Quilliam in presenting a brand of Islamic worship that would satisfy the visiting Muslim without irritating the Christian passer-by. The 1893 requalification of the Sunday "divine services" to "public lectures" denotes a growing understanding of the importance of publicly displaying a degree of Islamic orthodoxy, if not in practice (the Sunday religious services were held until 1908), at least in print, to get validation and patronage from the Islamic world.

129 The LMI caretaker in 1895 was James Nixon (*TC*, 21/08/1895, p.117). Although it is uncertain whether he was a convert, he gave public lectures at the Muslim Literary Society and took part in the Amateur Dramatic Society as well as the Institute's Annual Meetings from 1895 and 1896, and is named "Professor" in *The Crescent*. Nixon died in late 1896 and was buried in consecrated Anglican grounds. He was replaced as building caretaker by Mr. Jennings.

cap on top of them. You see a sofa in front of the window and a fireplace across the room, with a few chairs on either side, and a mirror above it, a few chairs on the right hand side and a pretty table in the centre, in addition to two pipe lamps above all of them.

There are six small plates decorating the walls. Three of them are [inscribed respectively with] "Truly religion with God is Islam" (ان الدين عند الله السلام), "There is no god but God" (لا اله الا الله), and "I believe in God ... [to] the Hereafter" (آمنت بالله الى آخره) written in the ta'līq style. The other three have photographs in them.

If you return to the corridor, leaving the room behind you, you will find the stairs on the left leading to the upper floor. Please go upstairs. We have arrived at the first floor, haven't we? You will come to another corridor. The window in the room to the right [36] overlooks the street.

This room is designated as a museum, in addition to serving the muezzin of Liverpool – our brother Mr. Arthur Hasan Radford – as the place to make the call to prayer every Sunday evening at 7 o'clock.

The contents of the room are no more than a few fish and cat skeletons, some stuffed birds and a few stones and ores of different minerals and suchlike. There are antique shops that sell similar items on Manchester Street in Liverpool and if you are familiar with the contents of a single display cabinet in these shops, then it would suffice to describe the objects in this room. To have the audacity to name a room that lacks historical or scientific objects a museum can only be explained by Quilliam being an attorney.

Exiting this small room with a sour expression, we return to the corridor and turn left. After walking past the staircase, we will come to another door on the left. This is the entrance to the room which Quilliam has named the Institute of Islamic Sciences (دار الفنون الإسلامية).[130] Let us enter and see what we will find. We have stepped inside. Apart from a school blackboard on the wall to the right, and two maps of England and Europe that are hanging on the wall across to the left, [37] we see chairs for pupils and a few wooden stools. That is the entirety of the room. To be able to describe this place to my respected readers properly, I would like to note the following: as our brother Mr. Quilliam became Muslim he is not going to send his eight children to Protestant missionary schools. He

---

130 Asmay uses the term Dār al-Funūn al-Islāmiyya, although it isn't used at the LMI. The section of the Institute that he describes here is the "Liverpool Muslim College", also called "Medrassah-i-Islamia" in *The Crescent* and *The Islamic World*.

wishes to educate them as Muslims and since it will be costly, even if he does not wish to send them to those schools, he has designated this room as a school and appointed a convert named Mr. Wilde on a £4 monthly salary as a teacher to educate his children. Other converts' children can also study here, which is very praiseworthy. However, instead of misleading brothers in faraway places by dubbing it an Islamic Institute, for the sake of verisimilitude, it should have been called a Muslim school. I have twice visited this room during class. I have seen that they do not teach anything other than elementary sciences in English. Although evening classes in Oriental languages have been advertised, it is said no one wanting to study or teach them could be found.

If only **[38]** the brothers and sisters-in-faith in Liverpool could study the Qur'an and *'Ilm-i ḥāl*,[131] a concise manual of Islamic faith, worship and ethics under a religious scholar one evening a week at this school it would be of great benefit (خـير).

Unfortunately, Mr. Quilliam has not taken this into consideration and paid heed to the similar recommendations of [other] well-intentioned Muslims. Even when this unworthy [author] suggested this, he said, "My intention is to do all that, but it is not time yet. First, we need to get an Oriental-style mosque with a minaret built, but I couldn't collect enough money yet for it. I have a debt of about £600."[132]

Although it is time that we should take our leave and go upstairs to the second floor, it is the residence of the old man, who works as a doorman or caretaker, but there is no point in doing that. We would do better to go downstairs.

When we descend the stairs that we came up earlier, we turn left and walk down the corridor. First there is a room designated as a classroom on the left, but it is not in use presently. Perhaps it is not yet needed. A small room next to it is supposedly dedicated to those who wish to make ablutions. After that we find a door in front of us with

---

131 The *'Ilm-i Ḥāl* genre was a persistent feature from the mid-sixteenth century onwards in the central Ottoman lands. These were primers in faith and practice directed at a lay audience, see D. Terzioğlu, "Where 'Ilm-i Ḥāl Meets Catechism: Islamic Manuals of Religious Instruction in the Ottoman Empire in the Age of Confessionalization", *Past & Present*, 220/1, August 2013, pp.79–114, https://doi.org/10.1093/pastj/gtt001.

132 Plans that were drawn up for a purpose-built mosque that was never built, see J.H. McGovern, *Lectures in Saracenic Architecture* (Liverpool: 1896–8), LPRO 726.2 MACG.

a sign hanging on it **[39]** that reads "There is no god but God and Muhammad is the Messenger of God" (لا اله الا الله محمد رسول الله) in *jali* style. This is the place that is designated as the mosque, which was the backyard of the house, with the side walls and the back wall raised a little and the ceiling is made into the shape of a camel's back [an open gable]. The gas pipes needed [inside the house] run through the walls as well as the ceiling and the lamps are attached to them.

You enter the room by descending two steps. On the wall where the [entrance] door is, there is a one-metre-high and two-metre-wide platform (محفل).[133] Facing the wall on the left side of the platform is an organ – meaning a keyboard with bellows – as large as an upright piano. In addition to that are three chairs and three lecterns – placed on one of them is an old English book.[134] In front of the stage are six rows with ten chairs in each. On each chair is placed a hymn book, which they call "hymns" [for short]. A large prayer mat is placed in the empty space behind these rows of chairs.[135] **[40]**

Gilded plates are hung on the wall [behind the platform] but I did not record their exact number. Two Ottoman flags are hung on the wall across (the door): one of them is red and the other is green. The space where the prayer mat is laid is the [designated] prayer place while the chairs are for listening to the sermon and reciting hymns.

Although there is a 'library' in our list of subsections it is premature

133 Although Asmay is facing a simple platform, he resorts to an Arabic term relating to the terminology of Ottoman mosques in his effort to compare the LMI's place of worship with mosques from the Islamic world. A *mahfil* is an elevated gallery dedicated to royalty or to women, or it can define the stage from which the muezzin calls to prayer and repeats the imam's refrains during prayers. The presence of a *mahfil* is not a mandatory requirement for a mosque, so Asmay doesn't appear to be disappointed that the platform isn't being used as such by the LMI.

134 According to Pool's account of his 1891 visit to the LMI this book was the Qur'an, see Pool, p.397. Dr Henry Martyn Clark who visited in the same year provides more detail, "At the west end, on a small platform, stands a table. On this is a very fine Damascene Koran-stand; by it is a velvet cushion, on the stand and cushion there are a couple of Korans in English (Sale), the bindings of which showed marks of usage." in Monro, p.6.

135 The two Christian accounts describe the prayer area as having been railed off in 1891, Pool, p.397; Monro, p.6: "[A]t the east end a small portion, about one-fifth of the whole, was railed off, if I may use the term, by benches placed across the room. The railed off portion was carpeted; on the carpet lay a white drugget spread when Namaz is performed. At the end which pointed Kiblawards, lay a prayer rug of medium size and at the end, also on the wall was a tablet of wood with the Kalima."

to write about it as there are not yet even a few books placed in a corner to constitute a makeshift library. Nonetheless I have my excuse for failing to provide any information on this. I would like to present as my excuse for including the library in my description as it appears in the Turkish translation of the advertisement that is regularly published in *The Crescent* newspaper.

ADVERTISEMENT
Liverpool Muslim Institute, and School, and Mosque
8, Brougham Terrace, West Derby Road. [41]
All Muslims are eligible to membership and to the privileges of
the institution.
The Mosque is open every day for Prayers – Jumma Namaz every
Friday.
Reading-room, Library and Museum open daily.
[Public lectures, which strangers are invited to attend, every
Sunday at 7pm.][136]
Explanatory works on Islam can be had from the Hon. Sec., or at
the Mosque.
There is also a Day and Boarding School for Muslim Boys, and
Day School for Girls; for particulars apply to the Hon. Sec.
Evening Classes in Oriental Languages.

Now what would persons from places outside Liverpool conclude after they keep reading the advertisement that contains this information in every issue of *The Crescent* newspaper, which has been published for years? I am sure they would believe it is true or at least very close to the truth.

After seeing it with my own eyes and being among them for thirty-three days and examining and inspecting every aspect in depth, this unworthy [author] would like to tell you the truth of the matter [42] that:

Muslims in general in Liverpool are not members of the elementary school that is named an institute (دار الفنون), which in reality is a small room where Mr. Quilliam's children study.

The mosque is not open for visitors every day let alone for worship.

Saying [we are holding] Friday prayers is only lip-service.

A lecture room and library has not come into existence. The [desultory] state of the museum has been mentioned above. The Day school is an

---

136 In the original advertisement but omitted by Asmay.

embellishment as is the case with the Friday prayers.

During my time there, I did not manage to ascertain who is supposed to be the [responsible] person to apply to for more details. If the person who is styled as "Honorary Secretary Omar Quilliam" is indeed one of Quilliam's sons, then he is an innocent [child] who is barely ten years old.[137] Writing that there are evening classes for Oriental languages is like putting one zero in front of another. Alas, how much do the events of our times suffer from the pens of English journalists and the speeches of their lawyers? They have the ability and power to make [43] a grain as small as a speck appear as big as a ladle. With our brother Mr. Quilliam being both a lawyer and a journalist, is it hard to imagine what he might be capable of, if we give it a little consideration?

Days and Style of Worship

Although the house that is designated as the mosque in Liverpool opens on Wednesdays, Fridays and Sundays at 7pm and closes after about an hour-and-a-half, I would like to note that Wednesdays and Fridays are not for worship but for discussion.[138] When a few and unemployed from among the male and female converts gather in the private members room on Wednesdays and Fridays, after asking each other, "How do you do?", which is used for "nasılsınız" [How are you?], followed by "It's a nice day", meaning "güzel gündür", they do not have anything left to discuss or say to each other. Yours truly has made sure that he was present in the room on these discussion days but has not heard anything that is akin to discussion other than the sound of the piano being played by fellow Muslim sister [44] Miss Nelson,[139] who knows how to play the piano, accompanied by the pretty voice of Miss Gibson. When Miss Gibson's delightful voice duets with Mr. Holehouse's deep and rugged voice one quite forgets one is in the discussion room of a mosque. I for one used to feel like I was in an opera theatre and can proudly say that I never failed to give them a round of applause, voicing my appreciation at the end.

When someone arrives in England, who is unfamiliar with her customs and moral character, the first thing that will catch his attention is

---

137 Asmay is confusing one of Quilliam's sons with his third cousin John Omar Quilliam (1853−97), cashier and general business manager in Quilliam's office, member of the LMI from 1891.

138 For a discussion of the development of Friday Prayer at the LMI see the Introduction.

139 Not as yet identified.

the girls' greater liberty and, if he rushes to judge them, he may start doubting their chastity. Over time, however, he will grow to understand that the surprisingly free attitude of English girls does not bring about the bad results one sees in [the rest of] Europe. Therefore it is worth noting that the convert sisters who play the piano, sing ballads and sometimes get up to do a few step dances [45] in front of the congregation, which I have witnessed a couple times, is not because of their loose manners but is part of their national customs. If you feel obligated to condemn this practice, I would simply direct you to address the venerable Mr. Quilliam directly but to ask nothing more than why he does make the discussion topic exclusively for male converts or – if female converts have to be present – limit it to those who are married.

Ritual prayers (نماز), or entreaty (نیاز), or acts of worship (عبادات), Friday sermons (خطابت), or admonition (وعظ), religious counsel (نصیحت) or hymn (الهی) recitation, or meetings, in brief, all this happens on Sundays in the room designated as the mosque. At 7pm, the congregation gathers at the private members room for the recitation of the Muhammadan call to prayer.

At 7 o'clock sharp our brother muezzin, Mr. Arthur Radford – the poor soul is deaf and has a slight lisp – recites the *adhān* in Arabic and then in English in front of the window in the room designated as the museum, which I mentioned above. It is the same *adhān* as we recite. I would like to provide the English version, which I noted during my stay there, as follows: [46]

Allah is great, Allah is great.
I bear witness there is no God, but God.
I bear witness that Mohamed is the prophet of God.
Come to prayers.
Come to Salvation.
Allah is Great.

Following the recitation of the honourable call to prayer, the person who will act as imam dons a fez. Mr. Nasrullah Warren, who is employed to teach Quilliam's children elementary chemistry, metallurgy, electricity, etc. for a £4 salary, stands in for Mr. Quilliam, who is with Nasrullah Khan's retinue in London, and acts as imam. Our brother Mr. Haschem Wilde, who is the preacher (خطیب),[140] also wears a Persian fur cap. The

---

140 Asmay refers to Wilde as the "preacher", using the term *khaṭīb*, i.e. the person

young lady Rosa Warren,[141] who is somewhat pretty and nonchalant, performs the duties of organist.

The imam, the preacher and the lady organist, whose voices call the congregation to the mosque and are heard everywhere [in the house], walk on to the podium [47] through a hidden door from the ablution room that I described above. The young lady sits on the chair at the organ while the imam and the preacher take their designated seats.

The congregation also enters and takes their seats in any of the six rows, after picking up the book of hymns, meaning *ilahī*,[142] placed on each.

Anyone who wishes takes his hat off and dons a fez. In any case they do not keep the hat on. Girls and women always keep their hats on.[143] When I was there, I observed that girls and ladies sat in the front rows with their hats on. A few had quite wide-brimmed straw hats on, which blocked the view of the front for the men behind. When everybody took their seats, holding their hymn books, the imam and the preacher would confer with each other [...] and the lady organist would leaf through her sheet music.

Their style of worship
Although it is certain that for the Muslim community (امّت محمّد) the Muhammadan call to prayer is recited to announce one of the five obligatory prayers (صلات خمسهء مفروضه), it is still not discernible which ritual prayer the honourable *adhān* is recited for [48] by the Liverpool Muslims, as it is always called at 7pm [on a Sunday] As Liverpool is in the North [of England], depending on the season its days and nights get much shorter or longer than Egypt's or Istanbul's. In early August, daylight lasts for about eighteen hours and I saw the dawn break about three hours after midnight. [During summer,] this means the *adhān* called at 7pm would be for *'aṣr* prayers. During the winter, however, an *adhān* at 7pm would be for *'ishā'* prayers. The same would also apply

---

providing the sermon (*khuṭba*) at the compulsory Friday congregational prayer (*jumū'a*). He assumes he is attending an equivalent, but on a Sunday. For further discussion, see the Introduction.

141 See Appendix 3 for biographical details.

142 Asmay uses a familiar Ottoman analogue to explain what a hymn is.

143 Here is an interesting example of cultural syncretism at the LMI. At Anglican church services, while men were always required to attend bare-headed, etiquette for women allowed them to keep their hats on. At the LMI "Sunday services", this habit was maintained. Although the men could don a fez at the LMI as a sign of their belonging to the Islamic *umma*, they removed it during liturgical moments.

for *maghrib* prayers depending on the time of year. In other words, the honourable call to prayer that is always done at 7pm does not apply to a certain ritual prayer – unless this is a special prayer of the followers of the Quilliamist way (طریقت کوئیلیامی)![144]

First the imam stands up and reads out aloud a page from the Qur'an in English, then he recites the following prayer[145] and the congregation [49] repeats it after him.

PRAYER[146]

O one only and true God, the Creator of the boundless infinity of space, who planted in the heavens the resplendent orb of the Sun to give us light by day, and the fair luminaries of the Moon and Stars by night, who in the magnitude of the unerring wisdom formed this world from nought and having made man planted him therein, and has sustained and protected the human race from the time of creation until now. We thy weak, erring and frail servants humbly approach thy throne to offer Thee adoration, to render thanks for thy great and tender mercies vouchsafed to us in the past, and to offer our petitions for a continuance of thy Divine protection and blessing. We praise Thee for that Thou hast created us and our ancestors who have been before us and the heavens as a covering, and hath caused water to descend from heaven, and thereby produced the fruits of the earth for our sustenance. We thank Thee for the revelation which Thou hast sent down to us by Thy holy prophet Mahomed, as a direction to the pious who be- [50] lieve in the mysteries of faith in order that they may have a knowledge of and observe the appointed

---

144 The term Asmay uses, translated here as "way", refers to a Sufi order (*ṭarīqat*), a number of which have in his view strayed from orthodox Sufi orders within Sunni Islam. See Introduction for details.

145 Reproduced from the English original, "A Jumma Prayer (As Offered In the Mosque at Liverpool by the Sheikh-ul-lslam of the British Isles.)" (*TC*, 20/03/1901, p.187). There are three differences between Asmay's version, presumably copied from a book of "Moslem liturgical prayers", separate to the LMI hymnal, which was in use ca. 1891 and the prayer reproduced ten years later in *The Crescent*. "Mahomed" is replaced by "Muhammad" – a more orthodox spelling of the name; an element of the final *du'ā* is left out by Asmay, or added later by Quilliam: "And Thine shall be the glory and dominion for ever", a reference to the Qur'an (55:27); to the final "Amen" is replaced in 1901 with an Arabic "Amin".

146 Asmay translates this as *du'ā* (supplication); the whole supplication is rendered into rhymed couplets.

times of prayer and distribute alms[147] out of what Thou hast bestowed on them and have a firm assurance in the life to come. We also pray Thee to protect and bless His Imperial Majesty Abdul-Hamid the Second, Sultan of Turkey, Caliph of the Faithful and Defender of Thy true faith, and also Her most gracious Majesty, Queen Victoria, sovereign of these realms, and His Highness Abdur-Rahman Khan, Ameer of Afghanistan and all Mussulman Sovereigns everywhere. Guide them with wisdom from on high, so that their official acts may be for the lasting benefit of the people committed to their care. We further pray Thee the most Merciful God to teach us words of prayer even as Thou taughtest them to Adam;[148] illumine our minds so that we can perceive at all times what Thou wouldst have us to do, so that whilst on earth we can follow Thy direction and when our time in this world is past, finally bring us to dwell with Thee in the glorious gardens of perpetual and eternal bliss.

Amen

[51-52-53: Translation of the prayer into Turkish by Asmay]

Following this supplication (دعا) the venerable Mr. Imam then sits down on his chair and leaves the respectable congregation to reflect for a moment on the spiritual ocean they dived into.

When he stands up again, he gives the number of one of the hymns from the hymnal. For example, he says, "Hymn N°2 which is about Chapter 91 of the Qur'an (والشـمس وضحاها) shall be recited."

The congregation rises from their seats and finds Hymn N°2 in their hymnals. Meanwhile the lady organist Miss Rosa Warren places her feet at the ready on the organ pedals. The page with the sheet music for Hymn N°2 being open, she starts [54] playing the organ while sight reading the musical notation. Although this organ is not as big as those in cathedrals, it is more than large enough for the gathering place or *salon* – which Mr. Quilliam calls a mosque – and its mournful sound resonates through the place.

At the imam's signal, the congregation of girls and children and old ladies and young men and old men with gravelly voices start singing Hymn N°2 in a touching way, while trying to keep up with the tempo of the organ.

---

147 Asmay translates this as *zakāt*.

148 Asmay adapts this phrase in his translation to a supplication to be taught the most beautiful names of God (*asmā' al-ḥusnā*) as opposed to the "words of prayers" in the original.

I must admit that when I was among the congregation, I got an elbow jab from the convert standing next to me for my bad singing. I had to lower my gruff voice and accompany the hymn by following [the words] with my eyes only. Even though the harmony of various voices accompanied by the organ soothes the soul I am unsure if it can direct the human mind to the spiritual realm.

I am so disappointed at being unable to note down the musical mode of it as I could not manage to obtain the sheet music for the hymn. However, I can tell you that it is quite similar to the melody of the "Oh, I love sheep" line in one of the famous comic operas, *La Mascotte*.[149] **[55]**

Hymn N°2 is provided word for word as follows:

BY THE SUN AND ITS
RISING BRIGHTNESS[150]
SURA 91 KORAN

Awake, my soul, and with the sun,
Thy daily course[151] of duty run;
Shake off dull sloth and early[152] rise,
To pay thy morning sacrifice.
Redeem thy miss-spent time that's past,
And live this day as if thy last;[153]
Improve thy talents[154] with due care,

---

149 Asmay, who has little to no knowledge of Protestant hymns, is comparing the LMI tune to *La Mascotte*, a successful comedy opera represented at the Théâtre des Bouffes-Parisiens (1880–9) that he may have attended during his stay in Paris. The lines that Asmay is mockingly comparing the hymn to include animal sounds: ("I love you more than my turkeys, when they do their sweet *gobble gobble gobble* / I love you more than my sheep, when each one goes *baa baa baa*").

150 Opening verse of Chapter 91, *Al-Shams*, George Sale's translation, *The Koran* (London: Frederick Warne, n.d.), p.582. Asmay mistakenly gives this as the title of Hymn No.2 when it is an indicator to read Chapter 91 before singing the hymn in question. The original text is *A Collection of Hymns Suitable for use at the Meetings of English Speaking Moslem Congregations* (Liverpool: T. Dobb & Co., 1892), p.4.

151 "Stage" in the original, C. Vincent et al, *The Hymnal Companion to the Book of Common Prayer with accompanying tunes*, 3rd edn. (London: Sampson Low, Marston & Co, 1890), No. 2, p.2.

152 "Joyful" in the original, Ibid.

153 "Thy precious time mis-spent redeem;/Each present day thy last esteem;" in the original, Ibid.

154 "Talent" in the original, Ibid.

For the great day thyself prepare.
Let all thy converse be sincere,
Thy conscience as the noon day clear;[155]
For the[156] all seeing God thy ways,
And all thy secret thoughts surveys.
By influence of the light divine,
Let thy own light in good works[157] shine;
Reflect all Heaven's propitious rays
In ardent love and cheerful praise.[158]

L.M.[159]

[56: Turkish translation of Hymn No2 by Nazmi Suat] [57]

The congregation quietens down, and everybody takes their seats. The organ falls silent too. Although one cannot know exactly how long the silence lasts without timing it, it would not be erroneous to estimate it as at least five minutes.

The venerable imam, Nasrullah Warren, rises from his seat and calls out another hymn number, for instance N°14. *Kurrrr....*[160] Rising from their seats, the congregation finds Hymn N°14 in the hymn book and the lady organist starts playing. The congregation begins singing the hymn as follows: [58]

---

155 "Thy conscience as the noontide clear;" in the original, Ibid.

156 "Think how" in the original, Ibid.

157 "In others" in the original, Ibid.

158 Only the first four stanzas out of ten in the original. Both of the hymns quoted, "By the Sun and Its Rising Brightness" and "Your Lord Best Knoweth", are translated by Nazmi Suat, an unidentified translator – perhaps a small-time poet himself – as he translated in metric form with an ABCB rhyme scheme. It is not retranslated here back into English but it is clear that Asmay wanted to convey a feeling of the ritual to his readers by commissioning the hymns' translation from Suat, whom he considered to be more poetically gifted than himself.

159 Asmay assumed these were the authors' initials. L.M. here means "Long Measure", indicating the number of syllables, a common practice in Protestant hymnals.

160 An Ottoman Turkish onomatopoeic word for the sound of thumbing through or riffling pages.

YOUR LORD BEST KNOWETH[161]
SURA 17 KORAN

My God! my father![162] while I stray
Far from my home on life's rough way,
O teach me from my heart to say
Thy will be done.
If Thou should'st call me to resign
What most I prize – it ne'er was mine
I only yield Thee what is Thine
Thy will be done.
Control[163] my will from day to day,
Blend it with Thine and take away
All that now makes it hard to say
Thy will be done.
And when on earth, I breathe no more
The prayer oft mixed with tears before,
I'll sing upon a happier shore
Thy will be done.[164]

MISS ELLIOTT.[165]

[59: Turkish translation of Miss Elliott's modified hymn by Nazmi Suat] [60]

Then they take their seats. After standing and sitting and singing hymns [repeatedly] for about an hour in this sequence, it is time for the preacher (خطيب).

When this unworthy [author] was there, the duty of preaching fell to

---

161 A phrase from Qur'an 17:84; Sale renders it as "Say, Every one acteth after his own manner, but your Lord best knoweth who is most truly directed in his way", *Koran*, pp.280-1.

162 Asmay removes the capital from "Father" present in the original LMI hymnal, *A Collection of Hymns*, p.12.

163 "Renew" in the original, C. Vincent et al, *Hymnal Companion*, No. 371, p.411.

164 Takes the first, fourth, sixth and seventh (final) stanzas of "My God, my Father, while I stray", Ibid.

165 Charlotte Elliott (1789–1871) was a writer of about 150 hymns and a poet; this was among her very best-known hymns. As was the case with the previous hymn, the second translator, Nazmi Suat, rendered this hymn into Ottoman Turkish rhyming couplets. It has not been retranslated here but omitted.

our brother Mr. Haschem Wilde.

The sermon (خطبه) does not begin with giving thanks to God or end with reminding the congregation about the injunction to uphold justice and benevolence (عدل و احسان امرينی). However, it starts with recitation of a verse from the Noble Qur'an and fulfils its purpose by giving an interpretation of it (تفسير), and he [the preacher] does so in a simple language that the congregation can understand, which is praiseworthy and should be applauded. I hope we can see the same in our mosques.

Nonetheless, all the four times I have attended the sermon, I was perplexed by not hearing anything except the preacher's attacks on Christianity in a harsh language.[166] I believe it would be more beneficial if the sermon was limited to talking about the virtues of Islam and directing this congregation of [61] new Muslims towards obeying and worshipping (عبادات) God and encouraging noble manners rather than criticizing Christianity in the name of Islam among the Christians [generally] and the Protestant priests, who certainly have influence on the people.

I have no doubt that the Quilliam group's publicly uttering such views that neither Islamic books nor Islamic scholars express using such strong language against Christianity will bring more harm than benefit.

I have heard things from a few Muslim intellectuals and a handful of Protestant priests that I was able to meet in Liverpool that confirmed the abovementioned opinion. I have, with great regret, watched some Christians walk in to see what this place is about and how Muslims perform prayers and observe the performance of the service, then grab their hats and quietly leave as the preacher's anti-Christian discourse becomes increasingly strident during the sermon.

I have an excuse for not being able to provide the text of at least one sermon in my pamphlet. Although I kindly asked Mr. Wilde several times for a copy of his sermon and told him I would like to publish it upon my return to Egypt and spread it among our brothers-in-faith he [62] did not accede to my request.

Later I learned that the venerable Mr. Quilliam, who refrains from

---

166 According to *The Crescent*: "On Sunday evening last, Bro. Professor H. Haschem Wilde lectured at the Mosque, his subject being 'Peace on Earth.' Bro. Professor Nasrullah Warren occupied the chair. Fully one half the number in attendance were strangers, who listened with unabated interest to the able discourse. Bro. Samih, notwithstanding he does not speak English fluently, understood so well the tenor of Bro. Wilde's remarks that he asked for a written copy thereof, in order to transmit a translation to his friends in the East." (*TC*, 24/07/1895, p.57).

presenting the truth [about the Institute] to the public but rather distorts it, would not give even a piece of paper [i.e. documentary evidence] to Muslims coming from the Orient to verify his work and, to be frank, because they are concerned about him.

In any case, let us go to the original source for the hymns that they sing. In the hymnal, along with the organ's musical accompaniment during the service in the venerable Mr. Quilliam's mosque, there are fifty-four hymns out of which fifteen are drawn verbatim from the Protestant book of hymns and psalms called "Common Prayer", used for regular [Protestant] services.

Hymn N°2 (provided above) is also the second hymn in *The [Hymnal Companion to the] Book of Common Prayer*, while Hymn N°14 is N°371 in the same volume. Although the original consists of **[63]** seven stanzas, the second and third [and fifth] stanzas are omitted.

In the Gospel of Matthew 6: 9–10, one reads: "This, then, is how you should pray. Our Father in heaven, hallowed be your name. Thy kingdom come, Thy will be done, on Earth as it is in heaven." The fourth lines (refrains) in Hymn 14, which is "Thy will be done", are taken exactly from this.

Whereas Hymn 11 in [Quilliam's] hymnal follows Psalm 127 word for word, "In vain we build unless the Lord/The fabric still sustain; Unless the Lord the city keep,/The watchman wakes in vain." and so on.[167]

Likewise, Hymns Nos. 13, 15, 18, 19, 20, 30, 32, 40, 43, 44 and 45 are taken from the [same hymnal companion] to the Protestant Book of Common Prayer.[168]

I would like to recommend [interested readers to refer to] the following book of the Protestant denomination: **[64]** *The Hymnal Companion*

---

167 Asmay is not quite right here. In fact, the precise wording is from "In Vain We Build Unless The Lord", based on Psalm 127, by Charles Wesley (1707–88), a Methodist leader whose older brother, John, founded the Methodist Church. The only exception is the phrase in the first line of the second stanza, replacing "trust our Father's love" with "trust in Allah's love". See *A Collection of Hymns*, pp.10–11.

168 In C. Vincent et al, *Hymnal Companion*, the respective hymn numbers are listed here in brackets after those in Quilliam's hymnal: 13 (20), 15 (565), 18 (247), 19 (274), 20 (579), 30 (54), 32 (222), 40 (350), 43 (295), 44 (279), 45 (241). A quick analysis shows that Quilliam's hymn selection here is ecumenical but reflects his Wesleyan upbringing: eleven of the hymns are Nonconformist while the remaining four are Anglican/Episcopalian. A full examination of Quilliam's adoption of these hymns for Islamic worship is beyond the scope of this study; Riordan Macnamara is, at the time of writing, undertaking such a study of the hymnal and of the LMI's liturgical documents, religious sources and references as part of his ongoing doctoral work at the University of Bourgogne, France.

to the Book of Common Prayer, third edition, revised and enlarged, 1890.

The sermon's completion signals the end of the service's performance, so everyone takes their leave. As the congregation leaves the mosque, the old caretaker hands out yesterday's *Crescent* newspaper to each. After 8.30pm, there is nobody left in the premises. The style of worship (عبادات) that has thus far been described and narrated was established and chosen by our friend Mr. Quilliam and resembles the Christian religious service performed in the Protestant churches to a tee, and is a Quilliamist innovation (بدئة كوئليامي), for he tries to fashion himself as a Luther to the Muslims. [That is, namely,] the verbatim replication of common Protestant prayers and erasing the phrases "Jesus Christ" and "Son of God" and replacing them with our Prophet Muhammed (صلى الله عليه وسلم) and presenting this to our English brothers and sisters-in Islam, who have found guidance, as Islamic worship (عبادات) and have them sing it accompanied by an organ in a place which is no different than a Protestant church. [65] Dear Mr. Quilliam, I do not know what the meaning of all this amounts to?

We think it more pertinent and fitting to leave [the] criticism and judgment [of this issue] to our honourable readers and to carry on with an account of our findings.

When Muslims from the East, who sometimes arrive in Liverpool, make sure they visit this house designated as a mosque in order to meet their new brothers-in-Islam, the converts kindly ask them to lead a prayer (صلات) according to the manner done in the Orient. As I opted to stay in London for a few days, one of my travel companions journeyed on ahead to Liverpool before me. During his visit to the mosque, he was asked by the convert brothers and sisters to act as the imam for the 7pm prayer (نماز). When he obliged them, he became quite upset because they did not know how to observe the conditions (شروط), essentials (اركان), or etiquette (اداب) of prayers (نماز). As making ablutions inside [the room] of a small house was difficult as such, especially for the women and girls, they formed the rows (صف) without ablution, and so on. The strange part is that while their hats remained on their heads, [66] they took their shoes off, showing their tiny [...] feet in socks to the congregation. What was even more peculiar is that out of respect for the fairer sex, they had the ladies take the front row and the men the back row, because these fair creatures were not able to prostrate (سجود), [i.e., perform] prostration (سجدة), due to their [brimmed] hats and [stiff] corsets, so they sat and

84

prostrated with their eyes while bowing their heads slightly, and various other similar [indicative] gestures happened.[169]

In my humble opinion, this evil consequence (وبال) and the responsibility for it lies squarely with our brother Mr. Quilliam, because it is incumbent upon him as president to teach or to facilitate the teaching of *'ilm-i ḥāl*, [namely] a concise manual of Islamic faith, worship and ethics to those whose hearts have been guided [to Islam].

Maulana Muhammed Barakatullah

He is a young Indian, chestnut-hued, with a slim, trim build, bespectacled, [and] high-spirited. He has been employed by the venerable Mr. Quilliam for £1 a week as his secretary and confidant over the last three years because he knows Persian, Arabic and English apart from his mother tongue of Urdu. Having studied Arabic and Persian at Indian madrasas, [67] he came to London with the hope of finding work in England. After leading a dog's life and picking up some English there, he gave himself up to Quilliam and caught his breath in Liverpool.

Indeed, his job consists of penning endless letters that talk about the growing success of and the subsequent need of financial assistance for the LMI and its Muslim community addressed to Arab, Persian, Afghan and Indian rulers of the Islamic world (امراء) in Arabic, Persian and Urdu. His additional job is to be introduced as the Mufti of Liverpool to Muslims from the Orient who come to visit the city.

He is supposedly teaching the converts the essentials (اركان), conditions (شروط), and etiquette (آداب) of Islam and advising them on the virtues and moral character of the Muslim *umma*.

In this unworthy [author]'s opinion, there is no need to fill up many pages to describe this respected personage. Before attributing eminence to his religious scholarship, to those who know the doctrinal carelessness of young persons who arrived in Europe at a young age and grew up there I would like to present *the* Maulana Barakatullah with the definite article and thereafter say no more.

---

169 Two months earlier, the Ottoman Consul of Liverpool Kenan Bey had also criticised the converts' collective prayer organisation to his superior: "the women are never veiled, and the English people's posture in prayer is so awkward that it spoils the required ensemble and gives the whole thing a bizarre effect." For him, religious services at the LMI are "baseless innovations" that are "contrary to the self-respect and religious sentiments of all good Muslims" (14/06/1895, BOA, HR.SFR.3 446/50, in Sharp, p.66).

He is well-mannered. He likes reading the newspapers, which is one of the characteristics of English upper classes, and following the political news. [68] His business card reads:

Muhammed Barakatullah al-Mawlawi
Professor of Oriental Languages at
The Liverpool Muslim Institute
Liverpool

He is poor. He needs every little penny. Perhaps against his better judgement, he has to pen letters requesting grants and donations from the wealthy and the rulers in the Islamic world[170] and defend Quilliam. A week before my return to Egypt when I read the chapter and section titles of this book to him and asked him if he had anything to say in this regard. He said it was true but that it would be harmful to publish this truth in the Muslim world. To conclude, shifting from a religious subject to politics, he tried to make Mr. Quilliam the Gladstone of Muslims in Britain.[171] The discussion ended as he was reminded that he was changing the subject and that this matter was entirely religious.

At Eid al-Adha last year, Turkish sailors from an Ottoman ship named *Mecca* gathered in Quilliam's mosque to perform the Eid prayers and [69] asked Maulana Barakatullah to lead the prayers as imam. Then when the venerable imam led the prayers with six *takbirs*, it is said they got upset and left the mosque without [sharing the traditional Eid] greetings. It is also said that a few times he led the [evening] *maghrib* prayer with four *rak'at*s [instead of three]. I was present when a

---

170 Asmay could have been told about Quilliam asking for donations through Barakatullah from Nafeesah Keep, as she had publicly accused Muslim leader Mohammed Webb in New York a few months earlier of similarly writing to Muslim benefactors in India and Turkey to collect subscriptions that, according to Keep, he was using for personal gain. N. Keep had, like in Liverpool, approached the Turkish consulate in Manhattan to voice her complaints, see Abd-Allah, p.247.

171 British statesman William E. Gladstone, who had served as Prime Minister for four terms stretching over a dozen years and retired from politics that same month, was an Evangelist, popular also among the non-Anglican Dissenters for his views on the importance of individual conscience in religious affairs. As a politician, he was a Liberal and advocated social mobility and inclusiveness beyond creed and class. For Barakatullah, Quilliam was a similar figure for Anglo-Muslims at the LMI and Muslim subjects of the British Empire, despite Quilliam's close connections with local Tory Democrats, see Y. Birt, "The Quilliams, Popular Conservatism and the New Trade Unionism in Liverpool", *Islamic Review - Special Edition*, 2018, pp.28–33, 61.

well-spoken Muslim brother jested to those who complainingly asked, "How can *maghrib* prayers be four *rak'ats*?" "Well, what you prayed at the Liverpool mosque was not a *maghrib* prayer but the 7 o'clock prayer that *his eminence* Quilliam has invented!"[172]

There are two letters of Maulana Barakatullah in the possession of this unworthy [author], one of which he wrote to express his disappointment at not meeting me in London when I had returned from Tunbridge Wells to Liverpool via London and I received it [the letter] in Liverpool. I received the other one recently, after my return to Egypt. In order to disclose the truth, I would like to present parts of them to our honourable readers for they both contain serious and true information regarding the situation of the Liverpool Muslims and about Mr. Quilliam.

This writer was unwilling to publish them. [70]

However I would like to present my rationale that after seeing a prominent person of a nation publicly share a letter, which he wrote to a person of secondary importance of another nation, during his speech in the name of proving X and disclosing the truth, followed by all the world press publishing it, I have been inspired by his action and decided that on balance it was better to publish them.[173]

The first letter is as follows:

عزيزي السيد... المصري

السلام عليكم. قد وصلني كتابكم الكريم بعد ساعة عشر من الصباح حين نزلت من حجرتي للطعام. فما وفقت سعادة زيارتكم مرة أخرى. يا اسفا على هذا الخسران فاني قد اردت ان أتكلم مع جنابكم على أشياء كثيرة.

انا أقول لكم شيئا غريبا وهو هذا؛ بان هذه المرأة "كيب" أرسلت كتابا طويلا الى حضرة دولتلو نصر الله ان ابن امير أفغانستان تتكلم فيه أشياء شنيعة مخالفة

---

172 For reasons of convenience, Quilliam preferred to fix the congregational prayer times instead of relying on astronomy. The Friday "Jumma" prayer, that is referred to in *The Crescent* as taking place "at the time of Isha Namaz on Fridays", was set at 9pm. This coincided, in the summer of 1895, with the time of the shorter evening prayer *maghrib*. Therefore, Muslims unaware of Quilliam's rearrangements would have come to pray *maghrib* and found themselves following a prayer of *'isha'*. See the Introduction for more detail.

173 In addition to translating this Arabic correspondence, Asmay adds glosses to his Ottoman Turkish translation in round brackets. These glosses are retained here with their original round brackets.

كويليم افئندى ومخالفتي أيضا وتقول كلانا وجلان لا عفة لهما ولا ديانة فيهما.

وتقـول بـان كويليـم ومحمـد بركـة اللـه كلاهـما يـزوران النسـاء في بيوتهـن ليـلا للفسـق [71]

والفجـور. وهـذه امـرأة تقـول حضرتكـم هـي مسـلمة. واللـه يعلـم انهـا كاذبـة فيـما

تقـول وقـد عملـت بالمعروف لهـا دائـما وكتبـت الى الهنـد وغـيره مـن حسـن ثنائهـا.

...ولنعم الجزاء هذا منها

واسـئلكم شـيئا آخـر وهـو ان المأمـول مـن حضرتكـم هـو تـرك بعـض الفصـول مـن

كتابكـم عـلى أحـوال المسـلمين في ليورپـول. مثـل الصلـوة بـلا وضـوء والمزامـير في المسـجد.

فـأني قـد علمـت كل واحـد مـن المسـلمين آداب الوضـوء وقلـت لهـم ان ياتـو المسـجد بعـد

الوضـوء في بيتـه. ووجـود الموسـيقى في قـرب المسـجد كان لعـدم قدرتنـا عـلى بنـاء المسـجد

ولكـن الآن قـد جائنـا اللـه بالخـير فنبنـي مسـجدا لايكـون فيـه شـيء مـن المزامـير. ولـو كتبتـم

هـذه الأشـياء في كتابكـم فعلـماء الـشرق يفتـون – كـما هـو عادتهـم- بكفـر هـؤلاء المسـلمين

في إنكلـترا. وهـذا يكـون ضررا للمسـلمين..... الى آخـره

في ١٥ اكست سنة ١٨٩٥ لندن

محمد بركة الله

It reads:

Dear Mr. ..... of Egypt

Greetings to you. At ten in the morning [72] when I got out of my lodgings and went downstairs for breakfast I received your honourable letters. Your happy visit [to me] failed to happen yet again. It is a pity I was unable to meet you especially because I wanted to discuss many things with you. I shall tell you something that is odd.

This woman named Keep (he refers to above-mentioned American lady Mrs. Nafeesa Keep) has sent a lengthy letter to His Highness, the Crown Prince of Afghanistan Nasrullah Khan, and wrote disparagingly of me and Quilliam Effendi in her missive.

She told him that both of us are irreligious and indecent and that we were visiting ladies in their houses at night for wantonness (فسـق) and debauchery.

This woman is telling you that she is Muslim. Obviously, what she is saying is a lie. I have always been kind to her. I wrote letters to India and other places in praise of her…. And this is what I get in return…. I would like to request one more thing from your eminence, which is that you leave out some of the sections from your book [73] on the state of the Muslims in Liverpool, for example prayer without ablution and an organ[174] in the mosque. I have taught each of the Muslims the manners of ablution and told them to come to the mosque after performing ablution at home. The presence of music in the proximity of the mosque was due to our inability to set up the mosque except with some musical instruments therein. (Please note the excuse!)

However, now that the Lord Almighty has blessed us with good things (he refers to the £2500 donated by the Crown Prince of Afghanistan) we will build a mosque and there will be nothing of the Psalms in it. If you write these things in your book, then the scholars of the Orient – as they always do – (please note) will give a legal opinion (فتوا) that the Muslims in England are infidels. And this will harm the Muslims…. (And so on.)

15 August 1895, London[175]
Muhammed Barakatullah

Extracts from his second letter, which he wrote from Liverpool to this unworthy one in Egypt, that should be included in this book are as follows: [74]

اخى وعزيزى...

بالحق ان الإسلام في ليورپول غريب وشيء يسير. ولكن وجوده في إنكلترا خير من عدمه بوجوه لا تخفى على حضرتكم.

اما منع الموسيقي عن الجامع وترك التغني فيه باسم العبادة فيكون عن قريب ان شاء الله تعالا حين يكمل بناء المسجد على آداب المسلمين...

ولا مؤاخذة عليكم لو كنتم في كتابكم بغاية الحرية و مسئلة ايراد الجمعية الإسلامية و مصاريفها لا تتعلق بنفسى أصلا. بل كل ذلك بيد كويليم افندى و ليس منصبى الا خدمة الجمعية و تعليم البيان ولا غير. انا احب ان تكتب حضرتكم في كتابكم باني عديم الذمة في

---

174 Literally, "flutes".

175 This letter was written just a few days after the Annual Meeting of the Liverpool Muslim Association of 1895 (see Appendix 2), and for Asmay's comments on this meeting see Chapter 5.

مسئلة ماليات الجمعية لان المسلمين اذا ارسلوا شيئا الى كويليم افندى لاحق لهم ان يسئلونى عن كيفية صرفه. لانى برىء الذمة فى هذا الباب... الى اخره

فى ١١ أكتوبر ستة ١٨٩٥ ليوريول
محمد بركة الله

[75]
Here is its translation:

Dear brother….

In truth, Islam in Liverpool is a strange and negligible matter. However, as you know yourself, its very existence in England is better than its absence.

Hopefully, banning music at the mosque and quitting singing under the rubric of worship will take place when the construction of a mosque built in accordance with Islamic custom is finalized. (How? Is this excuse even logical?)

You cannot be reproached for writing your book as you see fit. I bear no responsibility for the income or expenditure of the Liverpool Muslim Institute; perhaps all of it is in the hands of Mr. Quilliam. My only duties are to serve the LMI and teach the Qur'an (تعليـم البيـان). I would like to state for the record in your book that I have no responsibility (عديم الذمة) with regards to the finances of the LMI (he means to say he has no liability). In other words, if the Muslims send anything to Mr. Quilliam they have no right to ask me how it is spent. I cannot be [76] held responsible in this regard. (And so on….)

11 October 1895
Muhammed Barakatullah

Any further commentary on this subject should be considered superfluous as it is obvious that honourable readers would naturally take the parts worthy of critique from both letters provided above and [take them] into consideration. Criticism and judgment rest with our honourable readers.

4
COMMUNAL LIFE AT THE
LIVERPOOL MUSLIM INSTITUTE

Conversion (اهتدا)

Certainly, there is no ceremony like baptism or anything of that sort in order to enter the religion of Islam, regardless of which religion, or of no religion, or from any race or nation. For anyone to enter the religion of Islam, it suffices to recite the six fundamental articles of faith in Islam[176] if they affirm them in the heart.

I have not heard that the Liverpool Muslims were asked to do anything other than that in order to convert. [77]

On this matter I have heard from our brother Mr. Quilliam that [the names of] those who convert in Liverpool are written down in the a special logbook at the mosque that they have accepted Islam and [they would be asked to] sign underneath. Thereafter, publishing the name of the person who has converted in *The Crescent* would not be without benefits, as I have pointed out in good faith.

As I have also explained previously, I asked to see the logbook containing the names of the [convert] Muslims from the venerable president. I did not have the fortune to see it and had to make do with listening to Quilliam saying exasperatedly that "the total converts are about two hundred and the logbook is with the Crown Prince of Afghanistan, Nasrullah Khan."[177]

---

176 See footnote 116 above.

177 Quilliam also refused to show the logbook to the Christian missionary Dr Clark in his visit to the LMI in October 1891 (Monro, pp.19–21), but did allow a journalist from the *Liverpool Mercury* to examine the logbook (known as the "allegiance book"), the six-point pledge and the signature of a Christian priest who had recently converted to Islam (*LM*, 30/10/1891, p.6). References in *The Crescent* to an "allegiance book" that people accepting Islam at the LMI were required to sign only postdate Asmay's visit, see *TC*, 29/01/1896, p.491; 05/02/1896, p.503.

Marriage (نكاح)

The Liverpool Muslims' execution of the marriage contract is similar to the performance of the civil marriage in force in Britain and is as easy as drinking a glass of water. They are indeed the same. The only difference is that the civil marriage happens through the bride and groom along with their witnesses signing an official register to declare that they have accepted each other at the registrar's, which means an administrator or official of the town, [78] before two witnesses while the Quilliamist (كوئيليامـي) marriage happens by a man and his wife signing a special book along with their witnesses to declare that they have accepted each other at the Liverpool mosque before these witnesses.

It is up to our readers to consider if this constitutes a valid marriage contract according to the honourable Islamic law.

Polygamy (تعدد زوجات)

As it will not be hidden from insightful people, it is absolutely necessary to adopt a policy of good manners (ادب) to promote a goal, especially if women are involved. God forbid...

Dismissive (of the fact) that to spread the religion of Islam in the Christian world, and particularly in Britain, women should be taken into primary consideration and precipitating their mistrust should be avoided in all circumstances, Mr. Quilliam has spread polygamy, or the practice of marrying multiple wives.

He has practised it himself first by marrying a female convert while being married to his wife who has not converted yet. As I was told when I was in Liverpool, these women are living in different houses and cannot stand to see each other's faces out of intense jealousy. A married Indian man, [79] who is living in Manchester, also got married (عقد نكاح) at the Liverpool mosque to a female convert that he had met.[178]

Polygamy is illegal in Britain. Therefore, I would posit that it is justified to reproach Mr. Quilliam's boldness in this practice without paying due regard to the legal penalties given to bigamists and disregarding that the [legally unrecognized] second wife cannot [legally] inherit in the event of her husband's death, etc.

It should also be considered that this practice can especially foster jealousy among women, which in return may hamper the growth of Muslim

---

178 On 5th May 1895, Said Asha from Manchester married a young convert, Miss Annie Mariam Kearns, at the LMI before the Sunday service (*TC*, 08/05/1895, p.145).

society there, might it not?

If the English courts became aware of that polygamy is approved and practised in England, then one wonders if it would not be harmful for our brother Mr. Quilliam? Or should we argue that, as a lawyer, he can defend himself? In my humble opinion, that is not the salient issue, but rather that anything that impedes the good cause of spreading the religion should be avoided.

Cleanliness and Ablution (طهارت و غسل)

Through my research about [80] how it is practised among Liverpool Muslims I only managed to learn this much.

Among the English people, the relatively better off take a bath every morning. Those who can't afford to do so wash themselves when they get access to water, which means that they go around trying to stay as clean as possible. It is worth noting that the way their toilets are set up prevents the use of water in cleaning.

Eids

The Eids among the Liverpool Muslims are not confined to Eid al-Fitr and Eid al-Adha as Mr. Quilliam has increased them to three by adding to these two religious Eids the Eid of [Christ's] birth, which is called "Christmas".

With Eid al-Fitr and Eid al-Adha the whole thing would be over and done with after a morning gathering in the mosque to announce Eid's arrival to the brothers-in-faith.

However, at the Eid of the birth of our master Jesus, our friend Mr. Quilliam would throw parties for the congregation and for many Christian children at the mosque with lots of food and music. When I enquired of Mr. Quilliam as to what benefit might be expected from inviting people to the mosque to feast on Christmas Day, he [81] simply replied that, "We have to follow the national customs of the country."[179]

Last Christmas, his *eminence* Mr. Quilliam invited many children to the mosque and had a puppet show inside it to entertain them after the meal.

---

179 Asmay refuses the idea that a Christmas charity event at the LMI may be an adapt-
   ed form of *da'wa*, or propagation of the Islamic faith. However, these ventures
   were understood as such within the LMI. With money collected by the "Zacat
   Committee", this "Christmas Zacat Feast" indirectly aimed to show visitors and
   press "that Islam taught ... to be kind even to the poor and distressed followers of a
   corrupt and semi-idolatrous creed" (*TC*, 02/01/1895, p.8).

Burial of the Dead

For now, the brothers-in-faith in Liverpool, who pass on to the Permanent Abode, are buried in the Christian cemetery without having been washed or [had] (funeral) prayers [said for them]. However, according to English custom, they deliver speeches before the deceased's grave to praise his good deeds and ask for the Lord's mercy. The brothers-in-faith in Liverpool, whose souls have set off [to the Hereafter] and leave this world of tumult and turmoil behind, have all been buried in this manner.

When I asked Mr. Quilliam what prevents him from acquiring some land for Muslim graves that would enable them not to have to bury deceased Muslims in Christian graveyards he said:

> Yes, although we have some money to acquire some land for a Muslim cemetery, I am thinking about sorting it out in another way. There was an Ottoman warship that came here recently and, [82] because there was cholera in Liverpool at the time, thirty of their soldiers died as a result. Hence, the Ottoman government purchased a small plot of land and buried the deceased Muslims there. I am planning to acquire this land through correspondence with the relevant authorities to make it a cemetery for the Liverpool Muslims.[180]

In parenthesis, I would like add that, upon hearing this news of a [dedicated] plot of land where there is a Muslim cemetery from Quilliam, I inquired about its whereabouts to verify its existence, but no matter how much I enquired and searched I did not manage to get any information. It is a pity that a public charitable endowment (وقـف) that has been acquired with money from the public treasury (بيـت الـمال) of the Muslims, and which is direly needed, is lost. May those responsible for preserving *waqfs*, the charitable endowments of Islam suffer [the punishment] of their sins [for failing to do so].[181]

---

180 Quilliam may have been referring to an event dating back to ca. 1870 when thirty sailors from a Turkish frigate were buried in the Necropolis in Everton, see J. Salter, *The Asiatic in England: Sketches of Sixteen Years' Work Among The Orientals* (London: Seeley, Jackson and Halliday, 1873), p.160. The Necropolis was only a few minutes' walk from the Institute in Brougham Terrace.

181 Asmay is alluding to the "curse of *waqf*" – traditionally written in *waqf* charters – that curses anyone with eternal damnation if he or she fails to uphold the purposes for which the charitable endowment was established.

Divorce

Mr. Quilliam claims that so far, no divorce has ever taken place among the Liverpool Muslims. Even if it were to happen, the "divorce" method that is accepted by the English courts would suffice. Although what they call "separation", [83] meaning that husband and wife live separately, happened a couple of times it was resolved not through the court but through Quilliam's mediation and they were reunited.

As no dower (مهر) is agreed upon at the time of the marriage contract nothing would naturally be paid to the wife at the time of divorce.

Among the converts, I saw a woman whose name I cannot now recall and whose husband was Christian. For the record, when I decided to remind Quilliam that according to Islamic Law her separation would be required, he replied that, "It is impossible."

5
MR. QUILLIAM'S
CHARACTER ASSESSED

Mr. Quilliam's Disposition

Mr. Quilliam's disposition is very strange from beginning to end. Apart from noting that he is a commoner among his fellow countrymen, going into detail about his past or his biography is not going to be of any use [in answering this question] for us. **[84]** That said, I must give some details about his disposition after his guidance to Islam.

It is said that an Englishman on his deathbed will gather all his children to his bedside to tell them his last will and testament. "My dear children," he says, "earn money by legal means. In any case, earn money. Earn money. Mo…." And then he lets out his last breath.

It seems that our friend Mr. Quilliam has promised his conscience to adhere to this stricture and act in accordance with it, as there are no legal or illegal means that he has not resorted to in order to earn money. He has not shied away from nor hesitated to engage with various professions under different names. Today, as an attorney, Mr. Quilliam goes by William Henry Quilliam at his offices in 18 Manchester Street, Liverpool; as the proprietor and editor (المحرر)[182] of *The Crescent* newspaper, printed at 23 Elizabeth Street, he is W.H. Abdullah Quilliam; as the owner of the Liverpool Muslim Institute at 8 Brougham Terrace, West Derby Road, **[85]** he is William Henry Quilliam; and as the president of the Liverpool Muslim Institute and [leader of the] Liverpool Muslim community, he is Sheikh Abdullah Quilliam.

It is of documented and verified fact that in Christian year 1891, four years ago, he held two professions and names other than those mentioned above, although it was not long before the police intervened and cut Quilliam's earnings short. The first of these [interventions] was in

---

182 Literally, "the [sole or chief] writer". Quilliam was the named editor on the front page of *The Crescent*.

1891. The police were tipped off that an illegal place under the name of a private investigation office (كاشـف أسرار إداره سى) had been established and managed by someone named Mr. Smith. As establishing such a business violated police regulations, the above-mentioned office was raided and upon investigation it was discovered that the founder of the business was a person named Mr. Victor and that Mr. Victor was none other than dear William Henry Quilliam, and so he was caught. After further investigation and prosecution, the above-mentioned place was shut down and its agents were dispersed and Mr. Victor, in other words Quilliam, was released on bail and made to promise that he would never engage in such an illegal [86] occupation again.[183] This private investigation office would only ferret out family secrets. You may well ask what kind of family secrets? Well, things like finding out the whereabouts of a good wife, who listening to friendly advice has run away from home, or virtuous daughters, who – grabbing their umbrellas – left their paternal homes to elope with their fiancés, and fetching them home. Or finding out for suspicious husbands whether their wives are having amorous congress with their lovers and reporting them to said husbands. How [do you like that]?

Approximately four years ago, Mr. Quilliam was caught by the police [on a separate occasion], but he somehow managed to get himself out of this tight corner. This is how:

The police raided a brothel that opened in Liverpool, which is illegal under English law. They detained its managers, a couple, Mr. and Mrs. Cuss.[184] While they were in custody, they confessed that they were only tenants and that the real owner was Mr. Quilliam. Is it [87] necessary to reveal further details about this case?

After having gone to great expense to rent and furnish a house in the hopes of making money, our friend Quilliam committed the [additional] fault of deception to evade the law to make some profit, and then probably asked Allah to save him from the attention of the police. How about that?[185]

---

183 Operating a private detective agency *per se* was not a crime in Britain in the late nineteenth century, so it is unclear from Asmay's account exactly what precise crime Quilliam was allegedly guilty of without further corroborating evidence to ascertain the veracity of this claim. See H. Shpayer-Makov, "Revisiting the Detective Figure in Late Victorian and Edwardian Fiction: A View from the Perspective of Police History", *Law, Crime and History*, 1/2 (2011), pp.165–93.

184 Erroneously transliterated as قوسـت in the original.

185 Some of the details Asmay relates are garbled here, but as discussed in detail in the Introduction above, this does refer to a genuine case from 1891–2. A short biogra-

When I heard this prose epic from Liverpool's raconteurs, told in the local style, I was confounded by the path our virtuous Abdullah Quilliam Effendi had taken, who would hand out his business card that reads "Sheikh al-Islam of the City of Liverpool" (شـيخ الاسـلام در مدينـهء ليورپـول) to the Muslims.

Mr. Quilliam has a regard for the fairer sex as much as he loves money, so he made a name for himself in Liverpool: they say that once he sets his eyes on a dove, she cannot escape his clutches even if she flies away. Thanks to the generous assistance of Muslims, he has indulged in various "under-the-bed sheets"[186] shenanigans in Marrakesh. On holiday, he revels with coquettes on the Welsh moors and woods. Meanwhile, in Liverpool, he had quite a few days spent in this regard while switching between jobs. Abdullah Quilliam, who has come a long way but has not quite left behind his old wolfish ways, tried to steal away (آشـيرمق) a refugee girl (مهاجـره)[187] who caught his eye on the Galata Bridge during a visit to the Abode of Felicity [Istanbul] **[88]** but failed and returned home upset about it, as is related by his own community.

We Turks believe in the proverb that "A leader must be true in speech and true of heart." I wonder if we can apply it in Mr. Quilliam's case?

For our friend, the virtuous Sayyid Sheikh Mr. William Henry W. H. Victor Abdullah Quilliam Effendi, who is engaged in spreading the religion of Islam in a country like England and publicizes to the Muslim world that he presides over an Islamic association, changing colours according to his whims and desires by assuming various names, I believe cannot be regarded as being in harmony with the sacred task of spreading the religion of Islam.

It is common knowledge that every country, every kind of nation, assesses the disposition and character of someone who is going to take up a leadership role even in a regular job, and, in any case, tries to ensure that he is untainted and an upright person, let alone in the case of a religious leadership [role]! Obviously, those who come forward to spread the word of religion and teach noble Islamic ethics (مکارم الاخلاق) cannot succeed in their efforts unless they set a personal example to the people. Knowledge

---

phy of LMI member Mr. George F. Cuss is also in Appendix 3.

186 Literally, "under the tent".

187 Borrowed from Islamic history this usage started with the first loss of Ottoman territories in the eighteenth century. Following the Turco-Russian War (1877–8), Istanbul saw an influx of Muslim refugees from the Balkans and the Caucasus, fleeing Christian persecution.

(علم) without good deeds (عمل) is akin to a tree without fruit.

I refrain from writing more on it in the hope that **[89]** the few incidents presented above describe our brother Mr. Quilliam's disposition sufficiently for our dear readers. To the contrary, if I were to include the summary of the documents that are written by the hands of Liverpool male and female converts, and are still in my possession, in this book, then who knows how much our readers would be [further] surprised.

His Highness, the Crown Prince of Afghanistan, Nasrullah Khan's visit to the Liverpool Muslim Institute which took place when he came to see the city

For the Liverpool visit of His Highness with his entourage, there was an official welcoming ceremony. Mr. Quilliam was present there, attired in his Moroccan robes, with the extant male and female converts (whom he made sure were dressed up in bizarre costumes), as well as a considerable number of friends.

Although Mr. Quilliam and his group came uninvited, the official Liverpool troop of guards did not prevent them from walking up to the platform, **[90]** certainly as a gesture toward Islam or frankly to His Highness.[188]

As the carriage of His Highness pulled up at the station, Quilliam and his group chanted "*Allāhu akbar*" and Mr. Quilliam's little daughter and Miss Gibson from among the female converts, who works at the Liverpool flower market, presented bouquets of flowers they had prepared for His Highness when he stepped on to the platform.[189]

---

188 In fact, Quilliam met with the Lord Mayor to discuss arrangements the day before the Crown Prince's arrival, see *LM*, 10/06/1895, p.6.

189 According to the *Liverpool Daily Courier*: "[T]wo Mohammedan girls, who proved to be Abdullah Quilliam's two eldest daughters, Khadijah and Hanifa, and who were veiled in Muslim fashion, presented to his Highness a beautiful bouquet of flowers, formed into the shape of a Crescent, and a basket of flowers on which the same floral device had been interwoven, both of these bouquets being specially designed and manufactured by Miss Gibson and her sister, Mrs. Caralli, who are members of the local Moslem community." (*TC*, 19/06/1895, p.194) Quilliam pronounced a speech on behalf of the British Muslims, then bent to kiss the Amir's hand. The Shahzada withdrew his hand, saying: "Nay, it is for me to kiss the hand of the Sheikh. Religion is before all dignitaries". Quilliam stepped back and the muezzin cried out in Arabic: "Your brothers in Islam welcome you to Liverpool, O son of the great Ameer Abdur-Rahman Khan!" Then, in a well-prepared chorus, all the male Muslims shout the Profession of Faith: "*Allah Akbar, Allah Akbar, Allah Akbar, Hashadoa l'Allah illalha, Hashado anna Mahomedar rosul Allah*". Then the entire community, men, woman and children sing in unison : "*La Allah illalha,*

One of the Muslims present during this [ceremony] describes the strange costumes that the female converts had put on at Quilliam's direction to imply that they follow the Islamic dress code:

Some have wrapped a few metres of white cloth from their head reaching to their breasts only leaving their eyes and nostrils visible, while some others had a large piece of lace on their hats hanging down at the sides, stood like a bride in her wedding veil, and some in particular wrapped a big handkerchief around their mouths and noses.[190] Thus, [91] they proved to His Highness that they followed the Islamic dress code and showed to the people of Liverpool that this is how strangely Muslim women wear religious dress out on the street.

When His Highness graced the Liverpool mosque with his presence, i.e. the mosque that's described in Chapter 3 and the house that's called the Institute (دار الفنـون), to meet the male and female converts, he sat down for a while in the area that is dedicated to worship.

One of the specific peremptory precautions that Mr. Quilliam had

Moliomedar, rosul Allah.", the men waving banners, the ladies' handkerchiefs and the children clapping their hands." (Ibid.) These ostentatious efforts by the LMI converts looked for Afghani imperial favour as well as civic recognition. The gesture of Nasrullah refusing the honours of the Sheikh on the train platform is a well-staged re-enactment of the traditional Muslim social paradigm in which temporal leader's legitimacy depends on the validation of religious and spiritual authority. Symbolic recognition from political authorities such as the Afghan Amir was crucial for Quilliam to garner support from the Muslim world. Although Asmay castigated the theatrical and folkloric aspects of the LMI converts at the reception, he understood Quilliam's manoeuvre and hastened to undermine it: he surmises that the group was "uninvited" and implies that the converts feigned a stricter Islamic dress code to give Nasrullah Khan a false impression of the converts' commitment to orthodox Islam. By adopting this position, Asmay echoes with Liverpool Ottoman Consul Kenan Bey, who after witnessing this reception of the Amir, mocked the LMI members' "oriental" garb and their shouts of the *shahada* and "other cries inappropriate for the circumstance" (Letter from Kenan Bey to Rüstem Paşa, 18 June 1895, BOA, HR.SFR.3 446/50, cited in Sharp, p.68).

190 According to Nafeesah Keep, writing for *The Crescent*, upon arriving at the station, "we reached the carriage which had been set apart for the ladies' dressing-room. Here we ladies rearranged our veils, but we were not shrouded as the spectators had evidently surmised we should have been; white tulle crossed the brow and covered the head, then the fleecy folds were drawn over the lower part of the face, quite concealing the features but leaving the eyes uncovered." To those who asked if they had been told to cover their faces as a "concession to the Shahzada's prejudices", she answers that "we wore veils because we were Muslims...." (*TC*, 10/08/95, p.27)

taken was to make sure that this place did not reflect its usual arrangement by removing and hiding the organ and the chairs the day before and organizing the space like a Muslim place of worship.[191]

While inside the mosque, all male and female converts in addition to some Christians were introduced by Mr. Quilliam to His Highness and his uncles who were accompanying him. Maulana Barakatullah acted as interpreter.

As one of those present transcribed exactly the Persian conversation that took place (through Maulana Barakatullah's translation) between His Highness and his uncles and Quilliam, [92] this writer thought it fitting to present a few sentences of it for the amusement of our honourable readers.

Introducing one of the female converts, Mr. Quilliam said, "Miss Lily Ethel (اثيل)."

His Highness Nasrullah Khan asked, "What is her Muslim name?" (نام مسلمان نيش چيست؟)

After thinking for a while, Mr. Quilliam said one of the female Muslim names that came to his mind, which was Khadīja. It is Qādūjā, he replied.[192]

[His Highness replied,] "Very well. Praise be to Allah. I am very pleased that she is a Muslim now. She is better than us because we are sinners and our sister is not." خيلى خوبست. الحمد لله بسيار شادشديم. آنكه (اكنون مسلمان شده است. ازمابهتر است. زيرا ما كناهكار هستيم. خاهرما كناهكارنيست.

Meanwhile the uncles of His Highness remarked, "This Quilliam is quite hardworking and diligent, because it is difficult to spread the religion in a disbelieving country and among the infidels." (بسيار مجاهد و غيوراست اين كوبليام. زيرا ميان كفره درديار كفرستان اعلان اسلاميت مشكلست)

[93]

Mr. Quilliam then introduced someone as the butcher of the Liverpool Muslims, certainly because he had read in the papers that His Highness, the Crown Prince, had brought his own butcher and cook to England.

At the end of the reception, Mr. Quilliam presented His Highness, the Crown Prince, with a list that contained the names of the male and female converts. Just before he left the mosque, His Highness Nasrullah Khan, who was exceedingly pleased with this state of affairs, announced that £2500 had been gifted to the Liverpool Muslim Institute. Mr.

---

191 Like Asmay, Ottoman consul Kenan Bey was also scornful at the dissimulation of removing the organ from the Mosque, a sign for him of Quilliam's duplicity (Letter from Kenan Bey to Rüstem Paşa, op. cit.).

192 This misspelling is capturing Quilliam's mispronunciation of the name.

Quilliam, who was all ears at the announcement of this Islamic donation, said he was going to build a mosque in Nasrullah Khan's name in Liverpool with this money to which His Highness replied, "I find it more appropriate that you name it after my benefactor, my noble father, His Highness Abdur-Rahman Khan, who still is the ruler of Afghanistan," and said farewell to the mosque.[193] **[94]**

The copy of the list of names
Quilliam presented to His Highness

As I somehow procured the list of names that Mr. Quilliam presented to His Highness, it is important to reproduce it below. The persons whose names appear on the list could not be present during the reception (at the LMI). What is strange is that in general the bearers of these names are not converts. While some are originally Muslim (i.e. Muslim by birth), some happen to be Christians. Therefore, to indicate these distinctions, those who were absent during the reception [at LMI] are marked with غ and those who are Muslim by birth are marked with م, converts are marked with ه, and Christians are marked with خ.

Hereby is the list of names[194] presented by Mr. Quilliam to the

---

193 By comparison, note this rather laconic account by the official Afghan court historian: "In due course, the prince disembarked from the canal boat and headed for Liverpool by rail. At eight o'clock that day, he arrived at that city's station. A detachment of regular horse and foot were there to honor his arrival with music and they welcomed and saluted him. From the railway station, the prince made his luminous way by carriage to Newsham House, which is especially for royalty. When he alighted there, the shaykh al-Islam, 'Abd Allah Quilliam, a convert to Islam, who had come with all the converts of Liverpool to the rail station, greeted the prince and invited him to his home. At ten o'clock, the prince honoured him with a visit, met with him and his brother converts, and performed the evening (maghrib) prayer in their mosque led by the imam, Mawlana Barakat Allah Khan Hindi. The converts – men and women, young and old – were honoured by the Sublime Presence, and from the bottoms of their hearts praised him and offered prayers on his behalf. The prince lavished favors on one and all and donated 50,000 rupees for mosque construction." See R.D. McChesney and M.M. Khorrami (trans. and eds.), *The History of Afghanistan: Fayz Muhammad Katib Hazarah's Siraj al-tawarikh* (Brill: Leiden, 2013), 3 Vols, Vol. 3, Part III, pp.1406–7.

194 The list that Quilliam presents to Nasrullah is incomplete and sometimes erroneous. Although Asmay counts 33 male members and 44 females, his list only contains 32 and 35. In Asmay's text, we have put his original words in bold and added extra information on the LMI members gathered from *The Crescent* and various newspaper and genealogical sources. At the time of writing, this search for further biographical details is incomplete. The positions occupied at the LMI are

Crown Prince of Afghanistan Nasrullah Khan during his visit to the Liverpool mosque:

- **Essad Kenan Bey (Muslim), the Consul of the Sublime State of the Ottomans to Liverpool**
- **Sheikh Quilliam (Convert), the President** of the Liverpool Muslim Institute
- **Mr. W.** Abdur-Rahman **Holehouse (Convert), Mr. Quilliam's** step**father,** Treasurer of the LMI
- **Mr.** Syed **Hadi Hassan (Muslim) is Indian,** senior pupil of the Liverpool Muslim College, then *Legum Baccalaureus* in Roman Law (1895) from the Liverpool Victoria University, LMI Hon. Secretary 1895–6 and committee member, secretary of the Young Men's Society, before returning to Bhopal, India, in 1896
- **Mister Ali Hassan (Muslim) is Indian** from Bihar. LMI Delegate in May 1895, with Syed Hadi Hassan, to the London Anjuman-i-Islamia conference against the "Armenian agitators" **[95]**
- **Professor** Hedley Haschem **Wilde (Convert)** (1871–1912), former Hon. Secretary of the LMI, Headmaster of the Liverpool Muslim College
- **Professor** Mahomed **Barakatullah al-Mawlawi (Muslim) is Indian**
- **Professor** Henry Nasrullah **Warren (Convert),** (b. 1866), science analyst, LMI imam and librarian, son of Elizabeth Leylah, brother of Rosa
- **Mr.** Thomas Omar **Byrne,** Irish (1856–1901), LMI Hon. Secretary 1893–4 **(Convert)**
- **Mr.** George T. Djemal-ud-deen/Djem **Fletcher (Convert)**
- **Mr.** Arthur Hassan **Radford** (1861–1918), LMI muezzin **(Convert)**
- **Mr. Warren (Christian) (Convert)**
- **Mr. George** Selim **Evans,** former mariner **(Convert from Arminian or Wesleyan Methodist Christianity)**

those listed in the Annual Meetings of 1895 and 1896. For further analysis of the list, see Introduction.

- **Mr. Robby/**Robert Ahmad **Quilliam (Convert),**[195] b. 1879, William **Quilliam's son,** born to Hannah Johnson, his first wife
- **Mr. Willy/**William Henry Billal **Quilliam (Convert),** b. 1885. **He is his second son,** born to Hannah Johnson, his first wife
- **Mr. Henry** Mahomed **Quilliam (Convert),** b. 1888. **He is his third son,** born to Mary Lyon, his second wife
- **Mr. Freddy Quilliam,** son of Alfred Ali Quilliam **(Christian). He only comes to the (LMI) school on Sundays**
- **Mr. Percy Quilliam,** son of Alfred Ali Quilliam **(Christian) also (only comes to the (LMI) school on Sundays)**
- **Mr.** Sidney Charles **Dare,** b. 1855, Turkish bath masseur from Oldham Central Baths, **(Christian) also (only comes to the (LMI) school on Sundays)**
- **Mr. Harry Dare (Christian)**
- **Mr. Elliott (Christian)**
- **Mr. Dare (Christian)**
- **Mr. Charles Bazonett (Christian)**
- **Mr.** [William George Ismail] **Winter** (1839–1904) **(Christian),** organist at the Muslim Institute, treasurer of the Debating Society from 1901, vocal music teacher at the LMI from 1902, committee member of the Medina Home for Children. **[96]**
- **Mr. Alfred Quilliam is not officially a convert, but he attends the mosque.** Committee member of the LMI in 1895, named Ali Quilliam from 1896.
- **Mr.** J. Omar **Jones** from Wrexham, Wales, **(Convert). Absent**
- **Mr. Carsey (Convert) Absent**
- **Mr.** Ali **Mokaiesh,** b.1856, Syrian shipping merchant from Manchester, hon. Vice-President of the LMI from August 1895, LMI member with his brother Kamil. Bankrupt in 1896, left for Beirut, defended by Quilliam in Feb. 1896. **(Muslim) Absent**
- **Mr.** Said **Asha,** Manchester **(Christian).**[196] Absent

195 It is an arguable point as to whether Quilliam's children could be classed as converts *per se*. After all, given that Quilliam had converted privately in 1886 and declared his faith publicly the following year, even his oldest child, Robert Ahmed, was only seven in 1886 and was brought up as a Muslim from childhood. Any of Quilliam's children born after 1886 would have been introduced to Islam in early childhood.

196 Said Asha was not a convert but a Syrian trader based in Manchester. A few

- **Mr.** James **Lester** also **(is not officially a convert but he attends the mosque)**[197]
- **Mr.** Paul **Harrison**, from Manchester, **also (is not officially a convert but he attends the mosque)**[198]
- **Mr.** Isaac **Atkinson also (is not officially a convert but he attends the mosque).** Converted ca. 1897 and took the name Youssof.
- **Mr.** John **Curphey also (is not officially a convert but he attends the mosque).** From Southport, converted in 1895 and took the name Yehya.

33 male individuals in total

- **Mrs. Khadijah Holehouse, Quilliam's mother (Convert),** President of the LMI Ladies' Committee
- **Miss** Louisa **Hanifa Jones (Convert),** Secretary of LMI Ladies' Committee
- **Mrs.** Mariam **Lewis and her child (Convert),** sister of Lilian Cartwright
- **Mrs. Cartwright (Christian)**
- **Miss** Lilian Ayeesha **Cartwright (Convert),** assistant librarian
- **Miss Edith Wilson (Convert)** [97]
- **Miss** Emily Ameena **Thomas (Convert)**
- **Miss Hadwen and her daughter**
- **Miss** Rosa Elizabeth Augusta **Warren (Convert).** Music teacher, organist for the LMI, b. 1862.
- **Mrs.** Elizabeth **Warren,** widow, mother of Rosa and of Nasrullah, "Leylah" from 1890 **(Christian)**
- **Mrs. Dare (Christian)**
- **Miss Webb (Christian). Absent**
- **Mrs. Warren (Christian)**
- **Mrs. Nafeesah** Mary Theresa **Keep is American (Convert)**
- **Miss Maggie** Al-Djemela **Gibson,** florist

---

months before Asmay's visit, he married a young convert, Annie Mariam Kearns, at the LMI.

197 Asmay is mistaken: James Lester converted and took the name Djemal ud-deen in 1887.

198 John Harrison had converted and took the name Abdul-Haleem, ca. 1893.

- **Mrs. Mary** Lyon **Quilliam, Quilliam's** second **wife**
- **Miss Bessy/**Elizabeth Bessima Khadijah **Quilliam, her first daughter**[199]
- **Miss Hattie/**Harriet Hanifa Quilliam, her daughter[200]
- **Miss Ethel** Mariam **Quilliam,** b. 1885, **Mary's first daughter [98]**
- **Miss Lilly/**Lilian Ayeesha **Quilliam,** b. 1886, **her** [Mary's second] **daughter**
- **Miss** Florence **Zulikha Quilliam,** b. 1890, **her** [Mary's third] **daughter**
- **Miss Rogers (Christian)**
- **Miss Lizzy Rogers (Christian)**
- **Miss Anne Quilliam is 4 years old**
- **Miss Anne Dare is 3 years old**
- **Miss Cary (Christian). Absent**
- **Miss M. Cary (Christian). Absent**
- **Mrs.** Elizabeth Fatima **Cates (Convert). Absent.** Converted in 1887, d. 1900.
- **Miss O'Brien (Convert). Absent**
- **Miss Bark (Convert). Absent**
- **Mrs. Lester (Convert) Absent**
- **Mrs.** Leah Zulieka **Winter,** wife of W. Ismail Winter, and **her child** Dollie **(Convert). Absent**
- **Mrs.** Amy b. Ogden **Mokaiesh, (Convert). Absent.** Wife of Ali Mokaiesh, Manchester, b. 1866.
- **Mrs.** Leylah **Curphey (Convert). Absent**
- **Mrs.** Annie Mariam **Asha (Convert). Absent.** Wife of Said Asha from Manchester.

42 female individuals in total

According to this calculation, the population on the list that Mr. Quilliam presented to His Highness the Crown Prince and that is reproduced above is only seventy-five, **[99]** out of which five are Muslims by birth.

---

199 This is a mistake: Elizabeth Bessima Khadijah (or Cadijah) (b. 1881) was the second child and first daughter of Quilliam's legal wife Hannah.

200 This is a mistake: Harriet Hanifa Quilliam (b. 1883) was not Mary but Hannah's third child and second daughter.

The remaining population of seventy is not all converts, while some are children and mostly his (Quilliam's) family members. It is up to our dear readers to compare and analyse.

The monies Quilliam received on behalf of the Liverpool Muslim Institute

It is impossible to give a correct estimate of the monies Quilliam has received on behalf of the Liverpool Muslim Institute, as *The Crescent* newspaper, which is penned by him and merely serves as a means for the dissemination of his views, never publishes the accounts of the Liverpool Muslim Institute's funds or [details] how it is spent. While there are some who inquire about it, they can never get an accurate account [of it] from our virtuous Sheikh Abdullah Quilliam Effendi nor will they ever get one. The monies and sundries sent to Quilliam by the worldwide Muslim community (امت) to be spent for the good of the Liverpool Muslim Institute remain a secret. Quilliam contends, [100]

> What personal benefit did I acquire since my acceptance and declaration of Islam? I did not see anything but loss. I could not even cover the cost of the three houses that I have purchased for now under my own name on West Derby Road, yet, despite that, with future donations that would be expected to come from Islamic countries, I can demolish them and build a nice Oriental-style mosque of historical importance in their place in Liverpool and so create a place of worship for true Islam. Although some money came from India and I took some from Lagos, I had high hopes for Istanbul and Egypt. I have travelled to Istanbul with this idea in mind however I could not receive more than £400, which means that I could only cover my travel expenses. As for Egypt, I could not get a penny from there. The amount that I have received from Marrakech or other Islamic countries (بلاد اسلامية) is not impressive either. I intend to build a mosque with the £2500 that the Crown Prince of Afghanistan has gifted. In brief, I did not profit at all from accepting Islam and declaring it.

The truth is [101] that the huge amounts the Muslim *umma* donated and sent to Mr. Quilliam for the Liverpool Muslim Institute – without finding out how the land really lies – have vanished. I endeavoured through various means to ascertain where the donations came from and the total amount received in this regard. However, I could not find out about all of it. At least this part is certain, based on the letters I received from two honourable persons in Liverpool and a copy of the *Porcupine* newspaper, dated 16 November 1895, and published in Liverpool, which gave some information about it. Although it cannot be regarded as the [absolute] truth I find it important enough to reproduce below to give some idea to our dear readers.

In the letter that I received from an honourable Muslim in Liverpool, dated 22 October 1895, it is written as follows:

Recently, which was about one month ago … Effendi paid me a visit. Upon my asking, he identified and verified the various donations that Mr. Quilliam received as such: £2500 from the Crown Prince of Afghanistan, £2000 from Rangoon, Burma [Myanmar], **[102]** £1500 from India and £1000 from other places, which altogether amounts to £7000.[201] What is strange is that there are those who have kindly written requesting me to ask Quilliam how the above-mentioned amounts were spent and managed. I did not even succeed in seeing the grand sheikh, let alone asking him a question. Quilliam must have [gone] to the Isle of Man, as he has been spending time there over the past few weeks….

In the *Porcupine* newspaper, dated 16 November 1895, the incoming (donations) appear as follows:

Our friend Mr. Quilliam took £2000 from Muslims of Rangoon, £3000 from the Muslims of Hyderabad and Bombay, £2500 from the Crown Prince of Afghanistan, £2–3000 from Turkey, £2000 from the Muslims of Lagos in the Sahel of Africa….[202]

According to this calculation, even if we assume that the amount he reportedly got from Turkey is £2000, then the total [still] amounts to £11,500.

The letter sent by one of Mr. Quilliam's best men in Liverpool to me, **[103]** dated 13 December 1895, is more important and proclaims the truth. Therefore, I will provide a summary of it below before ending this discussion. Here is its brief translation:

---

201 Asmay mistakenly puts £8000 here.

202 The LPRO holds the largest yet incomplete run of the *Porcupine* (1860–1905); sadly this issue and year are missing.

I did not know about many aspects of Quilliam's character before. Now I know intimately that the goal of this man is none other than to take the wealth of the Muslims. They are saying he has so far received £10,000 from Islamic countries. The truth is that Muslims in Liverpool can never fully know the full sum of donations this person has gotten so far. It is a secret. How can the Liverpool Muslims learn about the finances of the Liverpool Muslim Institute? Quilliam keeps telling the community that he has lost lots of money since he accepted Islam. However, the truth lies [104] elsewhere.

Now that Mr. Quilliam has received the donations of Muslims, he has no fear of those who talk or write against him, because he calculates that the Muslims who sent donations to him live far from Liverpool in various parts of the globe. None of them knows what the others have donated to Quilliam. In any case, Quilliam possesses newspapers that will publish and spread lies to serve his personal interests.

I think there is no point in trying to find a solution to this deplorable affair. Indeed, the Muslims made a grave mistake in this matter, because they did not even ask Quilliam to give a basic accounting of the total donations they sent him. The odd thing is they send all the donations to Quilliam but would like to hold me to account [for them].[203]

In truth, I am none the wiser than them on this matter… so on and so forth.

It is certain that Quilliam has received donations from Islamic countries. However, how much the total truly amounts to is a matter of speculation. In my humble opinion, the total amount is not less than £8000, which is a handsome sum of [investment] capital for Mr. Quilliam. If he were to spend the generated income [of this capital] wisely, efficiently and honestly to aid [105] the impoverished among the converts, educating the Muslim children, and publishing Islamic books to spread the religion of Islam, then great achievements would have been accomplished and he would have been regarded among the entire Muslim *umma* and even in England as a truthful, tenacious and upright sheikh of respect and his

203 Unidentified. It seems highly unlikely that Quilliam's own stepfather and close ally, W. Abdur-Rahman Holehouse, who served as LMI Treasurer in this period would have written surreptitiously to Asmay.

name would have been remembered with glorification and veneration and he would have earned Allah's favour. However, it is with great sadness that I must inform you that he has regarded this capital of Islam as his personal wealth and does not care about anything other than following his own whims and desires.

Muhammed Shitta Bey, a black sheikh from among the Islamic scholars of Lagos in Nigeria,[204] one of the British colonies, was granted the Ottoman Order of the Third *Medjidie* by His Highness the Caliph in order to reward his efforts to raise money to build a mosque in the above-mentioned city. The Ottoman Foreign Office sent the said order to the Ottoman Embassy in London to be delivered to the said sheikh.

In order to send the above-mentioned order to the said sheikh, **[106]** the embassy, based on the assumption that Mr. Quilliam in Liverpool supposedly was in contact and had correspondence with Sheikh Muhammed Shitta, delivered it to Abdullah Quilliam through the Ottoman Consulate in Liverpool. Quilliam, who claimed to be in correspondence with and an acquaintance of Muhammed Shitta Effendi,[205] immediately announced in his paper that he would go to Lagos as a representative of the Caliphate, putting on his famous Marrakesh robe and donning a turban and getting to Lagos in no time with a green flag in hand. You see, the donations he received from the Muslims there was all down to this deceptive rumour that he arrived as the representative of the Caliph of the Muslims. When Mr. Quilliam described the overwhelming respect and esteem in which he was held by the Muslims of Lagos, he related that [they said], "Since you came here as the deputy of the Caliph of the Muslims, we will carry you over our heads all the way to Khartoum should you wish it so."

At the time, it never crossed my mind that his highness the sheikh would have another objective in saying that.

In issue no. 2149 of the *Sabah* newspaper published in Istanbul, the Lagos stories were reported with its well wishes.[206] **[107]** Pity the *Sabah*

---

204 Asmay mistakenly put "Sierra Leone" here.

205 In fact, the Ottoman archives confirm that Quilliam was in direct contact with Shitta Bey and that he did play an intermediary role with Yildiz. Received in February 1894, there's an undated letter from M. Shitta and Y. Shitta to Quilliam requesting that he present their petition to the caliph to award the former for the building of a mosque in Lagos. Quilliam is addressed as "Sheikh-ul-Islam, England" in the letter (BOA-Y. PRK. AZJ. 56/7).

206 Literally, "prayers".

writer, unaware that his sky is cloudy [his view is clouded], who goes on to [try to] observe the sun with binoculars.

Although Mr. Quilliam came up with the idea to build and open an orphanage for illegitimate children,[207] who are left at the gates of hospitals and churches, to gather them, teach them and make them Muslims after which they would be sent off to Istanbul [to be educated] with the financial support of the [Ottoman] government. He requested the monies required for this task from some senior officials but could not get anything other than the reply, "May Allah help raise [them]",[208] and [so he] gave up on his idea. As if the Muslim *umma* sees any good in the legitimate children of Europe, yet he is expecting good to come of their children born out of wedlock!

An Assessment

By staying in Liverpool, this author had the chance to get to know and learn about Mr. Quilliam, his family members, a few ragamuffins hired by him, and about the fifteen commoners he gathered around him, and examine and observe their manners and behaviours in depth. Therefore, I would like to express to my dear readers that my conscience is clear about the things I have noted down and written so far.

I am sure that I have not written down anything [108] that is contrary to the truth. During my stay in Liverpool, I have received nothing but kindness and respect from Quilliam himself and the Quillamists (كوئيلياميســتلر). My objective has been to set out the facts. I read out this booklet's contents [and section headers] to them as well, which I had prepared there, and asked them to point out if there was any element of it that was not factual. All of them affirmed that my words were true but that publishing them in the Islamic countries would be risky. Yet even if the truth is bitter, it should be tasted; indeed, publishing it would be [a good deed that would bring] great reward (اجـر عظيـم). As a respected person from among them has pointed out [above], Mr. Quilliam no longer fears anyone. The Muslim *umma* of which he is a member of will not be able to claim back the monies that they sent him because he failed to spend them in the way of spreading the religion of Islam. So long

---

207 Literally, "natural" or "of nature". Asmay employs an obsolete euphemism here to avoid using the harsher term "illegitimate".

208 A formulaic Turkish expression of well-wishes for one's own children or those of others.

as there are means such as *The Crescent*, Quilliam can use this paper to spread as many lies as he likes through the Muslim countries.

Today, one of the distinguished people from among the Muslims kindly has invited the American Mrs. Nafeesa Keep, the poor woman whose name I also have mentioned above, to Egypt and invited [to host] her in his house, thus attaining **[109]** great reward through this deed of offering protection to an old and helpless female convert. Quilliam's convert father Mr. Holehouse had beaten her up with his shoes, kicking her out of the publishing house because she was informing Muslims in the Orient about their doings. They held a meeting in the mosque to expel her back to America; published the next day, *The Crescent* newspaper was full of lies, see under "Annual Meeting of the Liverpool Muslim Association".²⁰⁹ This author was present on the said day and date in Liverpool and thus I knew the truth very well. These lies that Quilliam has published in *The Crescent* were translated and published in most Muslim newspapers under 'Islamic Affairs' in the good faith that it was true. In *Servet-i Fünun*'s newspaper supplement, page 235, and in *Ceride-i Askeriye*, 8 September 1313/[1895],²¹⁰ no. 26, page 7, and *Sabah* newspaper and others, these lies were quoted as if they were true. Such a degree of Muslim naivete in this day and age cannot be excused. In the name of spreading the religion, a vagabond convert should only be able to con Muslims once at most. Mr. Quilliam has been taking advantage of their credulity by duping the Muslim *umma* for the last eight to nine years and it seems that at this rate he will keep on doing so. The responsibility of this sin (وبال) lies **[110]** with those Muslim writers who hold back [from saying] the truth. The Muslim scholars should know that Quilliam – who borrows from Protestant styles of worship and calls it Islamic worship and has made Muslim convert brothers and sisters pray (صلات) with music for the past eight years – has not taken the right path. Our venerable scholars should consider that writing booklets about the truth and the way of Muslim worship to spread it among the new Muslims is a more rewarding deed than writing about the Islamic schools that only exist nominally like the Jabriyya or the Māturīdīs. The Islamic society in Liverpool, and spreading the religion and endowments (اوقاف) should have been subjected to legal regulation. Muslims born in England, or at least Muslims living in England for business or other purposes from the

---

209 *TC*, 14/08/1895, pp.115-17, excerpts reproduced in Appendix 2.
210 Asmay mistakenly puts 1311/[1893] here.

places from which donations in cash are received such as India or Afghanistan, should have been permanent members of the society. The Ottoman Consul of Liverpool, who is the representative of the Sublime State of the Ottomans and the Holy Islamic Caliphate, should have attended the society at least for their grand meeting [annual meeting] to assess the annual income and expenses and improvements before it is published in *The Crescent* with his own decision and attestation (شهادة). [111]

The donations received should have been and ought, in the future, be accounted for; the real estate (عقارات)[211] that would be purchased in Liverpool or other places as the need arises should be acquired in the name of Islamic charity (أوقاف إسلاميه) and should be registered as such with the government offices. As the founder, Mr. Quilliam should have been the board member of these charities and a certain share of their income should have been given to him as the *waqf* manager and president and the rest should have been spent for the education of Muslim children. Male and female converts, who have become destitute, hungry and helpless, should have been helped. At least one Muslim legal scholar (فقيه) should have been a part of the society to teach the converts about the religion and the Qur'an, and lead the funeral prayers. A concise manual of Islamic faith, worship and ethics (علم حال) should have been made available and handed out to those who are converting. So long as Mr. Quilliam and his family remain Muslims, the right to manage and lead [the *waqf*] should been passed down from one generation to the next through the eldest child,[212] or else the society should elect a faithful president through consensus by a majority vote so that an Islamic society and the properties (عقارات) of Islam[213] can have an enduring presence. Unfortunately, none of this exists in Liverpool at the moment. Whatever exists now [112] shall persist so long as Mr. Quilliam is alive, but at the time of his death it shall be buried along with his body. And all this shall be forgotten and there will not be a grave for the cause of Quilliam among the Muslims.[214]

---

211 In the context of charitable endowments, this means both income-generating properties i.e. commercial lettings, or land, i.e. for a graveyard.

212 Probably an allusion to an old legal position for charitable endowments that the founder could leave the right to be president or a board member to his child, subject to certain conditions.

213 Charitable endowments belong to the Muslim public and hence to Islam.

214 These are prophetic words from Asmay as Quilliam was buried in an unmarked plot in Brookwood Cemetery near Woking in Surrey and was largely forgotten among British Muslims until a revival of interest in him from the 1970s onwards,

أفمـن زيـن لـه سـوء عملـه فـرآه حسـناً فـإن اللـه يضـل مـن يشـاء ويهـدى مـن يشـاء فـلا تذهـب نفسـك عليهـم حـسرات ان اللـه عليـم بمـا يصنعـون

As for those whose evil actions have been made to seem beautiful, God misleads whom He wants and guides whom He wants, so do not destroy yourself through them. God is All-Knowing about what they are doing.[215]

THE END

Cairo, Egypt, 26 Sha'bān 1313/10 February 1896

---

see Y. Birt, "Preachers, Patriots and Islamists: Contemporary British Muslims and the Afterlives of Abdullah Quilliam" in J. Gilham and R. Geaves (eds), *Victorian Muslim* (London: Hurst, 2017), pp.135–42.

215 Qur'an 35:8.

APPENDIXES

APPENDIX 1
RELATED DOCUMENTS FROM THE OTTOMAN ARCHIVES

Letter from Mary Theresa Nafeesa Keep to Sultan Abdulhamid II, Liverpool, England

August 3, 1895

By the hand of

His Imperial Majesty's Consul General, Liverpool,

This letter is respectfully submitted

To

His Imperial Majesty

Abdul-Hamid Second,

Sultan of Turkey,

Caliph of the Faithful and

Defender of the True Faith

In the year 1893, I began to study Islam. In the U.S.A appeared a man[216] who professed to teach this true Faith, but not one of the people who listened to him learned one prayer or ablution. I never heard the Moslem prayers; I never saw the Moslem ablutions performed in America.

I learned that Islam was established and flourished in England. I asked to be affiliated with the Liverpool Muslim Society. I am a member of this Society. I was broken-hearted over the false teaching of Islam in America.

In February 1895, I came to Liverpool. I lived upon my own money until June 13, 1895. Since that date W. H. Abdullah Quilliam (Sheik-

---

216 Alexander Russell Webb (1846–1916), the first prominent Anglo-American convert to Islam in 1888, a Muslim missionary, diplomat and newspaper publisher.

ul-Islam) has sent me Ten (10) Shillings each week. I have to pay for my lodging, food and medicine –I am starving –I have worked for W.H. Abdullah Quilliam in the "Crescent" Office, sometimes eight, sometimes ten, twelve, fourteen, even eighteen… [hours].

True Moslems who come here from the Orient tell me that true Islam is not taught and is not practiced in the so-called "Mosque" in Liverpool.

I have seen two (2) women stand shoulder to shoulder on the prayer carpet with the men, when the prayers were finished, one (1) young woman always let some one of the men fasten her shoes on her feet for her. I objected to this.[217]

I saw this same young woman kiss two (2) of the young men in the so-called "Mosque". I objected to this. But the "Sheik-ul-Islam" says we cannot have Islam in England exactly as it is in the Orient. – I am of middle age and very active –

I am called a thoroughly good speaker and writer of the English language – I speak German – I speak French, and read French, well enough to translate it into good English.

I want to reach a country where the people are true Muslims. I want to learn the Moslem prayers and ablutions. I want to live and die amongst true Believers.

My fortune is gone, my husband is dead, I have no children, I have no money, my health is broken fighting against the false teachers of Islam in America and in England: therefore I pray your gracious Majesty help me to find a home, among your gracious Majesty's loyal subjects, where I may earn enough money to feed and clothe myself properly.

Wishing your gracious Majesty long life and every blessing, I have the

---

217 A month earlier, Keep had been highly impressed by Afghan Amir Nasrallah Khan's attitude towards women at the LMI, that she associated with lofty Islamic morals. In an account of the visit that she penned for *The Crescent*, she asserts that "[Prophet] Mohammed made it a rule that Mussulmans shall not speak to a married woman who is not in the company of her husband." (10/07/1895, p.28).

honor to subscribe myself your Majesty's

Most respectful Petitioner,
Nafeesah M. T. Keep

From the Consul General of Liverpool to the Ministry of Foreign Affairs of the Ottoman Empire: BOA-Y.A.HUS 335/83.

The Sublime Porte, the Office of Foreign Affairs,
Secretarial Office

The copy of correspondence dated 6 August 1895 with
Liverpool Consulate General

This humble person [the consul-general of Liverpool] received a petition from a lady named Nafeesah Keep, who lives in Liverpool, in order to convey it to His Imperial Majesty, who is the Caliph. This petition is submitted to your exalted Ministry in a written form. The transmission of the above-mentioned petition to the higher authorities is bound to your sublime opinion.

From the Minister of Foreign Affairs to the Grand Vizier: BOA-Y.A.HUS 335/83.

The Sublime Porte, The Office of Foreign Affairs,
Secretarial Office
No: 2721

To His Excellency, the Grand Vizier,
This is the petition of your humble servant,

The petition of a lady named Nafeesah Keep, who requests relocation to a territory where the ordinances of Islam are properly enforced, to live a life and wants to become a subject of the sultan since Islam, reportedly, was neither appropriately explained nor implemented in the place that is used as a mosque in Liverpool (and where she serves), and asks for help due to poverty, is presented with the correspondence of the consulate of the above-mentioned city, dated 6 August [18]95 and numbered 105 as well as with the original of the petition and its translation. In this matter, the command belongs to him who commands all.

10 Rabī' al-Awwal 1313 / 19 August 1895

The Minister of Foreign Affairs

From the Grand Vizier to the Sultan: BOA-Y.A.HUS 335/83.

The Sublime Porte, The Office of Grand Vizier,

Secretary of the Imperial Council

No: 629

The official document of the Ministry of Foreign Affairs that contains the petition (to His Imperial Majesty) of a lady named Nafeesah Keep; who serves in the place that is used as a mosque in Liverpool, wants to become a subject of the Sultan, and asks for help due to poverty, with the correspondence of the consulate of the above-mentioned city, the original of the petition and its translation, is presented in order to be considered by your Highness.

Date: 14 Rabī' al-Awwal 1313 / 23 August 1895

The Grand Vizier

Said [Mehmed Said Pasha]

The Translation of the Petition of Nafeesah Keep: BOA-Y.A.HUS 335/83.

There are two very minor changes from the original petition and its translation into Ottoman Turkish.

– The Ottoman translation does not include "Sheikh-ul-Islam" for Quilliam but says Cemaat-i İslamiyye şeyhi (i.e. the sheikh of the Islamic group) Abdullah Quilliam Efendi (the original text does not include Abdullah Efendi)

– The translation does not specify the name of Quilliam's office (Crescent Office) but gives the same information for the rest

The Book Ban: BOA-HR.TH. 212/61.

The Sublime Porte, from the Ministry of
Internal Affairs
To the Ministry of Foreign Affairs

His Excellency,

The books of "Liverpool Müslümanlığı", "Tore Ermiya", "Makale-i Islamiye" and "Rivayet-i Sultan Selim" are prohibited to enter the domains of the Ottoman Empire because they contain harmful contents. According to this decree, the exalted ministry, by informing necessary bureaus and provinces, must fulfil what is required. In this matter, the command belongs to him who commands all.[218]

Date: 10 Muharram 1316/19 Mayıs 1314
[31 May 1898]
The Minister of Internal Affairs
Mehmed Memduh

---

218 I.e., authority is delegated to those Ottoman officials tasked with enforcing the ban by stopping the importation of Asmay's book into the imperial domains.

APPENDIX 2
ANNUAL REPORTS OF THE LIVERPOOL MUSLIM INSTITUTE, 1895-6
(EXCERPTS)

Like all philanthropic societies in the United Kingdom, the Liverpool Muslim Institute gathered once a year to discuss the events and decisions of the past year and elect board members. Publication of the Annual Meetings in *The Crescent* and *The Islamic World* served a promotional purpose: by highlighting the Institute's public and private events in terms of an annual "progression" of Islam on the British Isles, the aim was to encourage a constant, even growing, flow of donations to support its work.

The 1895 and 1896 Annual Reports are shaped as responses to Mary T. Nafeesa Keep's damaging endeavour to alert the Ottoman authorities to what she saw as Quilliam's mismanagement of the donations received and the lax mores at the LMI, and to Yusuf Samih Asmay's additional attacks on the unorthodoxy of religious practices, compounded with an exposure of Sheikh Quilliam's personal misconduct. What follows are extracts from these two Annual Meetings, which aim to defend the Institute's reputation and *raison d'être*, the proper management of the donations received from abroad, and its policies.

Annual Meeting of the Liverpool Muslim Association, 1895
[115] The Annual Meeting of the Liverpool Muslim Association was held on Monday evening, the 12th [August 1895] inst., in the Mosque, West Derby Road, Liverpool.

Bro. W. H. Abdullah Quilliam, Sheikh ul-Islam of the British Isles, presided, and there was a large attendance of members.

Letters of apology for non-attendance were read from Brothers his Honour Essad Bey, Ottoman Consul-General at Liverpool, J. Omar Jones of Chester, Hughes Quilliam of Fairhaven (uncle of the president), J. H. Duckworth of Accrington, J. Omar Quilliam, and R. Ahmed Quilliam Bey, both of whom were in the Isle of Man, and Professor Wilde, who was away on his holidays, and others.

The Hon. Secretary (Bro. Syed Hadi Hassan), read the notice convening the meeting.

The President congratulated the members on the success which had crowned their efforts during the past year, and the steady increase of membership. He sympathetically alluded to the death of Mahomed Shitta Bey of Lagos, one of the Vice-Presidents of the Society, which occurred on the anniversary of the consecration of the Mosque he had erected at his own expense, and also to the deaths of five of the members of the Liverpool Society which had occurred during the year. In continuation he said – A brighter chapter in the history of the movement was the visit of the Highness of the Shahzada, Prince Nasrullah Khan, second son of the Ameer of Afghanistan to Liverpool, his attendance with his entire suite at the Mosque for prayers, his inspection of the Mosque and schools, and his munificent gift of £2,500 to the funds of the Institution, out of which sum we have already purchased our present premises, so that where we now stand is our own property, consecrated to the worship of the One Only True God and the glory of His Holy Prophet in all perpetuity. We shall make a number of alterations and improvements **[116]** in these premises, so as to better fit them for use as a school and Muslim Institution and thus give permanence to the establishment of Islam in the British Isles, as well as erecting a handsome little Mosque on the site of the buildings within a few yards from this spot which we purchased some years ago, partly with the money sent us from the brethren in Rangoon. As time goes on, if further funds are entrusted to us, we shall purchase the intervening houses, and thus erect a handsome pile of buildings on this spot, which will be an ornament to the City of Liverpool and a glory to Islam. In conclusion, let me remind you that as Muslims we ought to remember that we are all members of one family. "Verily, the true believers are brethren," are the inspired words of the Koran, and this principle should be acted up to in everyday life by all Muslims. An injury to one Muslim is an injury to all; differences of opinion, honest differences, may arise between us, but we must give each brother and each sister credit for good intentions. Circumstances may arise when the conduct of a person professing Islam may be blameable and not conducive to the welfare of the general community, in such a case the matter must be laid before the governing officers of the body, and they must decide the question, if necessary the decision of the whole united body of the members may be taken, and when that has been given it must be taken as final, and be obeyed. We cannot allow the harmony of the family to be upset by one discordant element. There is no room in Islam for the profligate, the traducer, the slanderer and backbiter, the evil-minded, the unjustly suspicious, and the self-aggrandiser. The place of such an one is not amongst us.[219] Islam condemns in no unmeasured terms such conduct, and the perpetrator thereof cannot be a true Muslim. No amount of mere profession can constitute a person a Muslim, there must be the consistent practice of Islamic virtues, "Actions speak louder than words." To the Muslim his religion is his life, and in his life he must exemplify the faith that is in him, "We live in deeds not words." (Applause).

The meeting then proceeded to the election of officers, the following being unanimously chosen:– President, Bro. Sheikh Abdullah Quilliam (re-elected for the eighth year in continuous succession); hon. vice presidents, his Excellency Emin Bey, his Excellency Zekki Pasha, his Excellency I[brahim] Hakki Bey, his Honour Col. Ahmed Bey, all of Constantinople, his Honour Mahmoud Essad, Judge of the tribunal at Smyrna, his Honour Mahmoud Salem, Judge of the Mixed Tribunal at Egypt, Professor Mir Aulad Ali, Mustapha Karsa (Manchester), Ali Mokaiesh (Manchester), his Highness the Nawab Hassan Sarwar Jung Bahadoor of Hyderabad, Syed Mahomed Ali (Fategarh), Peer Mahomed Aliarakia (Bombay), his Honour Sir Syed Ameer Ali, Judge of the High Court (Calcutta), A. H. Moolah Dawood (Rangoon, Burmah), A. H. Musa Khan (Perth, Australia), J. M. H. Good (Cape Colony), Hajee J. Omar Chamberlain (Transvaal), Mahomed Sanussi (Sierra Leone), Yusuffu Shitta Bey (Lagos), his Excellency Sidi Mahomed Torres (Morocco), his Honour Essad Kenan Bey (Ottoman Consul at Liverpool), his Honour J. Loutfy Bey (Barcelona), and his Excellency Djavid Bey (Caimacan de Cos); hon. secretary, Bro. T. Omar Byrne; treasurer, Bro. W. Abdur-Rahman Holehouse (re-elected); librarian, Bro. Professor H. Nasrullah Warren; assistant librarian, Sister Lilian Ayeesha Cartwright (re-elected); committee, Bros. Syed Hadi Hassan, A. Hassan Radford (re-elected), Alfred Quilliam, and Sister Mrs. Mariam Lewis. Ladies committee – President, Sister Mrs Kadijah Holehouse (re-elected); secretary, Sister L. Hanifa Jones (re-elected); committee, Sister Mrs. Fatima E. Cates (re-elected), Sister Mrs. Mariam Quilliam, Sister Miss E. Amina Thomas (re-elected),

219 An indirect reference to Nafeesa Keep, who had been expelled prior to this meeting. Asmay witnessed her expulsion, see his account in Chapter 3 above.

Sister Miss M. Gibson, and sister Miss Rose Warren. Auditors, Bros. Professor H. Haschem Wilde, Moulvie Mahomed Barakat-Ullah, and G. Selim Evans, [117] Muezzins, Bros A. Hassan Radford, R[obert] Ahmed Quilliam Bey, and Billal Quilliam. Trustees of the Zacat funds, Sheikh Quilliam, W. A. R. Holehouse, professors Warren Wilde, and Barakat-Ullah. Keeper of the building, J. Nixon.

It was unanimously resolved to request his Majesty Abdur-Rahman Khan, Ameer of Afghanistan, and his Highness Prince Nasrullah Khan, the Shahzada, to become patrons of the Institution.

Votes of thanks to the officers of the previous year for their services during their term of office, and to the Sheikh-ul-Islam for presiding, terminated the extremely harmonious proceedings.[220]

Annual Meeting of the Liverpool Muslim Institute, 1896

[842] The tenth annual meeting of the Liverpool Muslim Institute was held on Monday evening, the 22nd June, in the lecture hall of the Institution. Sheikh W. H. Abdullah Quilliam, Sheikh-ul-Islam of the British Isles, presided, and there was an excellent attendance of members....

Sheikh Abdullah Quilliam, who on rising was received with great applause, said – We met to-day under very auspicious circumstances. Just prior to our last annual meeting we had to take the unpleasant but necessary step of suspending from all the privileges of the institution an individual who claimed to have become a Muslim in another land, but who by actions – which ever speak louder than words – had shown that the lip-profession of our faith was strangely inconsistent with her conduct.[221] From the time when we took that painful but necessary step until now, not one discordant note has sounded in our midst, and for the last official year we have truly been one family united together in fraternal bonds....

Our Increase
Twenty-one persons have joined our Institution during the past twelve months: of these fourteen were converts from Christianity, the remaining seven were born Muslims. We have had one death during the year.... This year has been a light one in that respect, and thus contrasts favourably with previous ones. Since 1887 no less than twenty-three of our members have died, a very large percentage indeed. The reason for this is, however,

---

220 *TC*, 14/08/1895, pp.115–17.
221 Another indirect reference to Nafeesa Keep.

not difficult to be understood. Those who become Muslims from conviction are almost all cases persons of mature age. In some instances quite elderly people have embraced the faith. [...] **[843]**

The Shahzada's Gift
This time last year we had the honour and the pleasure of a visit from his Highness Prince Nasrullah Khan, second son of his Majesty Abdur-Rahman Khan, the Ameer of Afghanistan, who bore with him as a gift to us from his enlightened and munificent father the sum of £2500. This money was handed to me without condition of any kind. I deemed its investment a sacred trust for the establishment of Islam on a permanent footing in this country, and after earnest consultation with the other officers of our Institution we decided to apply it as follows:—

For the purchase of our present premises, No. 8, Brougham Terrace, to which we are attached by many ties of historic and other associations, including all the legal expenses of the transfer, etc., a sum not to exceed...£750

In structural alterations upon the premises so as to rebuild the lecture hall, provide a playground for the school, fit up additional schoolrooms and provide a suitable small Mosque, a sum not to exceed...£650

To pay off the mortgage upon the premises, Nos. 11 and 12 Brougham Terrace, previously purchased by us for £1400 out of the money sent us from Rangoon and from Sierra Leone, a sum not exceeding...£750

To expand in structural alterations on these later mentioned premises as to enable us to have our printing office, and also a Khan for visiting Muslims, and living rooms for the Imaum of the Mosque, all upon the premises, No. 12, Brougham Terrace, and for furnishing these rooms, etc., a sum not exceeding...£200

Leaving a balance for miscellaneous expenditure, the relief of distressed Muslims, printing and publishing explanatory pamphlets, salaries, etc., of...£150

Or a total of...£2500

(Applause). These were our estimates; our balance sheet to-day will show how we have endeavoured to carry this out, and the exact amounts that we have expended under these various headings. [...]

Presents for the Ameer

We felt that such munificence from so illustrious a monarch merited the most assiduous attention to the comfort of his son, consequently several members of our association placed their time and efforts at his disposal were in almost constant attendance upon him and his suite at Dorchester House. The Sheikh-ul-Islam travelled seventeen times to London and back, and remained there for many days at a time; Moulvi Mahomed Barakat-Ullah we placed at their disposal for nearly two months; Professor Nasrullah Warren came up twice; R[obert] Ahmed Quilliam Bey, George Quilliam and his assistant, and L. Hanifa Jones, once each; and Bro. J. Omar Quilliam went on journeys to Bradford and Halifax to purchase articles required for the suite. In addition to this we presented an illuminated address, and also an electric lighted breast-pin to the Shahzada and a magnificent gold English-made watch to the Ameer. A full account of our expenditure on these items appears in the balance sheet.

The Purchase of 8 Brougham Terrace

We succeeded in purchasing these premises, and as soon as they became our own the work of alteration and improvement at once commenced. This was no light undertaking. The lecture hall was rebuilt and extended, a spacious room fitted up as a Mosque for daily services, the large hall being used for special festivals, such as the Great and Lesser Eids; a beautiful *Mihrab* erected; a playground with latrines, swings, &c., provided at the rear of the premises, for the use of the school. The whole of the premises were drained according [844] to the latest scientific improvements, under the supervision of the Corporation authorities; tanks and lavatories for the performance of the necessary *Wudu* erected; photographic, chemistry, electrical and metallurgical laboratories constructed and fitted up with a full set of chemicals, crucibles, furnaces, electrical and other apparatus; a retiring room and lavatories for ladies, &c. A handsome vestibule door with an ornamental plate glass panel has been fitted into the entrance hall, and countless other small improvements added, which are far too numerous to mention. Two brethren deserve special mention in connection with these alterations at the Mosque and school, namely, Mr. J. H. McGovern, F.L.A.S., who designed the Moorish arches and superintended all the technical details of the work, and Mr. W. Abdur-Rahman Holehouse, who not only acted as clerk of the works, but also worked most arduously and untiringly at these alterations (loud applause). [...] In commemoration of the visit of the Shahzada, a tablet has been inserted in the south-western wall, which reads thus:–

LECTURE HALL

Reconstructed November, 1895, at the expense of the
SHAHZADA,
SON OF THE AMEER OF AFGHANISTAN

W. H. ABDULLAH QUILLIAM,
Sheikh-ul-Islam of the British Isles.

J. H. MCGOVERN, F.L.A.S.,
Architect.
W. A. R. HOLEHOUSE, Clerk of the Works.

Another inscription in gold letters, in both English and Arabic, will be placed on the specially prepared tablet at the front of the room used as a Mosque, and facing the platform of the lecture hall, and will give the dates – in both English and Muslim chronology – on which Islam was first preached in England, the removal to these premises, the visit of the Shahzada, the munificence of the Ameer, and the re-building of the lecture hall, &c. (Applause.)

The Khan, Master's Residence and Printing Works
The work on these premises could not be commenced until after the expiration of the tenancy of the occupier of No. 12. He leaves at the end of this month, and then we shall at once commence operations. We have already purchased a quantity of furniture for the premises. The details of all this expenditure appear in the accounts, and the auditors have examined the vouchers for the same.

The Muslim College
The scholastic work has been ably conducted under the headmastership of Bro. Professor H. Haschem Wilde, and the pupils have made substantial and satisfactory progress. Our senior pupil, Mr. S[yed] H[adi]

Hassan, who is studying for the bar, has recently successfully passed the last but one of his examinations, and is now preparing for his final examinations. When he leaves us I am sure the best wishes of all his Liverpool brethren will go with him for his success in the profession he has adopted (applause). At the beginning of this year we were fortunate enough to secure the services of Professor Mustapha Khalil Bey, formerly of Damascus, and since then he has been of great assistance to Bro. Wilde. He is acquainted not only with Arabic and Turkish but also speaks French, German, and English, and already the fruits of his labours can be seen in the progress that the children had made in French under his careful tuition. Bro. Professor H. Nasrullah Warren kindly offered about fifteen months ago to conduct a chemistry class in connection with the college. We gladly accepted his generous offer, and since then he has not only taught the pupils of the college but also taken two evening classes as well, one for chemistry and the other for electricity. Our learned brother gives his valuable services to our institution, and it is to such public spirit as this that our Society owes much of its success. Let it be clearly demonstrated that the [845] English Muslims have adopted the faith not for personal advantage but because they believe it to be true, and the world will then know how to appreciate these courageous men and women who have boldly made a stand for truth. And here, if I may be permitted to digress for a minute from the immediate subject under consideration, let me say that it behoves us to be very careful in our selection of officers for this Institution. Islam is on its trial in England, and the slightest mistake will be made much of by its enemies. For the last nine years we have been passing through the testing furnace. The flames have driven off the dross but the action of the refining fires (applause). At the inception of Islam we were visited by all kinds of sorts and conditions of men. The curious came to gratify their curiosity; the lover of novelty to seek for something new; the faddist to air his particular crank (laughter); some came because they thought there was money to be made out of it – we quickly undeceived them on that score (renewed laughter); other thoughts it a step-ladder by which they might mount to fame, only to discover that their schemes of personal aggrandisement were incompatible with the teachings of Islam. In short, just as when the prophet Dawood fled from Saul to the cave of Adullam, and there then congregated around him everyone who was dissatisfied, and all who had a grievance, so a number of these "cranks" came around us. We had to discriminate very carefully amongst these people to winnow the chaff from the wheat, to distinguish the sheep from the goats. We filtered them (laughter); those who were worth having we spoke to in a kind and conciliatory manner and endeavoured to show them the beauties of Islam, and succeeded in obtaining some of them as converts to the faith; the others we let go their own sweet way. [...] (Applause)[222]

[858] As soon as our alterations at the Mosque were completed we decided to further extend the influence and usefulness of this institution by holding a series of evening classes, at which instruction would be given at a small charge to all who desired to avail themselves of the same. Our objects in doing this were multiple. First and foremost, to carry out the cardinal principle of Islam, to do good deeds to all, irrespective of sex, creed, race or nationality (applause); secondly, to demonstrate to the world that our faith was the patron and not the enemy of science, literature, and art; thirdly, to widen the sphere of our influence and remove prejudice, and, fourthly, if possible, to induce those who might join these classes to take an interest in this institution – to let them see what manner of people we were – in the hope that the spirit of enquiry might be engendered in their breasts... (great applause). The formation of classes required suitable teachers, and these I am pleased to say we found in our midst, from among our own brethren. I question very much if any other religious society of its size in the British Isles could have found so many brethren who were not only willing but also capable of giving instruction in so many arts, sciences, and languages as we have in our institution. [...]

The first evening class was one for instruction in photography and photometry, and is under the management of Bro. J. Hardisty Yates. This class meets every Tuesday evening and numbers, I think, about thirteen or fourteen members. My eldest son, [Robert] Ahmed, acts as financial secretary for the class, and Mr. A. Ward as treasurer. They subscribe a certain amount each quarter and apply their funds for the purpose of purchasing chemicals and photographic apparatus. Another very successful class is that for instruction in the French language. It is managed by Bro. Mustapha Khalil Bey, and is continually receiving fresh additional pupils. [...] Classes for the study of chemistry and electricity are held every Thursday evening in the laboratory, and are conducted by Bro.

222   *TC*, 01/07/1896, pp.842–5.

Professor H. Nasrullah Warren. [...] **[859]** [I]n the future form those able scientists, Pros. Warren and Dr. S. Kleeman. Mr. J. H. McGovern, F.L.A.S., has promised to commence a class for drawing, both freehand and architectural, and also for building instruction. Our Secretary will take one for shorthand, and we hope soon to be able to arrange, if not for classes, at any rate for lectures upon the sciences of astronomy and geology. The secretarial work in connection with the College is quite distinct from the work of the secretary to the Institution, and has been conducted very successfully by Bros. J. Omar Quilliam and J. H. McGovern, to both of whom our thanks are also due (applause). [...] **[860]**²²³

Our Literature
During the past year our weekly journal the *Crescent*, has been enlarged, and it and our monthly magazine, the *Islamic World*, have both been regularly issued and have obtained a gradual steady increase of circulation. A book of mine, entitled "Studies in Islam," has also been printed and is now in the hands of the binders, and should have been ready for issue prior to this meeting. I question very much if any journal of its size has anything like the world-wide circulation of our journals...

We are on the exchange list of quite one hundred foreign journals and magazines published in the following languages:– English, French, German, Dutch, Russian, Spanish, Bulgarian, Arabic, Turkish, Persian, Roumanian, Malay, Gujerati, Urdu and Bengalee. Many of these journals are bi-lingual, and scarcely a week passes without an extract from one or another of our journals being **[875]** quoted in some other publication. I regard this as one of the most important features of our work. Standing upon this platform once a week, my voice only reaches the ears of a certain necessarily limited number of persons, some of whom come merely out of idle curiosity and are never seen by us again. Although the importance of the lecture work is very great and must not be minimised or discountenanced and has been the undoubted means of bringing many converts into the faith, yet the printed matter we issue is read by hundreds and thousands every week. What is heard at a lecture is only retained in the memory for a time, but what is published and circulated remains ever in print, to be read and re-read over and over again. While we are asleep even, the silent witness still may be being pursued by numbers of persons in distant lands.

---

223   *TC*, 08/07/1896, pp.858–60.

Therefore I trust you will all properly recognise and appreciate this feature of our work. Financially it is a loss, and I am afraid will remain as such for a considerable period yet, but this is a contingency that we must boldly face and be prepared to meet (applause). The detailed account of the printers' and other wages in connection with our publications, the cost of paper, printer's ink, stereotype and other blocks, postages, &c., all appears in the cash books and balance sheets, and will doubtless be commented upon by the auditors. It takes two clerks in my office the greater part of three days each week to make up, address, stamp, and mail these journals. Their salaries do not appear in the accounts, as I pay them out of my own pocket. If I did not do so, the debit balance against the Institution would be increased by at least £60 each year. [..] [876]²²⁴

[T]he light of Islamic truth is breaking in portions of the earth which until recently those of other faiths had regarded as their own peculiar strongholds. The Christian clerics are beginning to recognise this fact. It has been a very rude awakening for them (laughter). So long as they could get their followers to believe that Islam was a moribund religion, based upon imposture, they sat at their case and quietly chuckled. The first efforts to establish Islam in this country were regarded and stigmatised by them as the foolish efforts of a lunatic, and I was regarded as a fit subject for a strait jacket and incarceration in a cell in an asylum for imbeciles. The simple existence of a Muslim Society in England mainly composed of Englishmen, however, focused attention upon the principles of the religion. It caused enquiries to be made, and then the consistent and regular progress of Islam throughout the world began to be noted, and enquiries discovered that things were not as they had been represented, that Islam was a living faith, standing on the vantage ground of simplicity and truth (applause). [...]

I fear that our Muslim brethren throughout the world do not thoroughly appreciate their own strength. It is high time they did so. We are numerically and socially the most compact religious body in the world. United under a trusted leader we could bid defiance to any [893] combination of Christian sects or countries. They talk of the union of Christendom. It is a good phrase, but will never be ought else. But the union of Islam might easily become an accomplished fact. The differ-

224 *TC*, 15/07/1896, pp.874-7.

ences of our schools of thought are so slight that they should soon be smothered over and adjusted. Even the question of Sunnee and Shia is, after all, more of a political than a religious difference. Islam teaches that in things essential there must be unity, and every Muslim – be he Hanifee, Malaké, Shafi, or Hanbalee, be he Sunnee, Shia, or Wahabee – all agree that God is one and Mahomed is His Prophet. In things doubtful Islam gives liberty of thought, and in all things it inculcates charity and forbearance. "Let there be no violence in religion," are the inspired words of the Koran, luminously standing forward as though they were written in letters of living light upon the pages of the sacred volume (applause). I call upon our brethren throughout the world to promote such an union! The Muslim's first duty is to God and Islam. The first thing necessary in order to bring about the crowning victory of Islam in the world is to carry out in its absolute entirety and in its fullest sense the immortal truth, "Verily the True Believers are brethren." Let no Muslim be even a consenting, much less an assisting party to the injury of another Muslim by a stranger to the faith. This is Muslim law; let it be equally Muslim practice (applause).[225]

This [matter of Muslim solidarity] is not and has never been a question of politics with me. It is purely and solely a question of religion. I decline to stand dumb and see Muslim set against Muslim in fratricidal strife, embroiled in a quarrel for which there is no cause, at the bidding of any *Giaour* or nation of *Giaours*.[226] The person who would cowardly hold his peace on such an occasion I regard as unworthy of the name of a man and a True-Believer. I believe in the complete union of Islam, and of all Muslim peoples; for this I pray, for this I work and this I believe will yet be accomplished. In England we enjoy the blessed privilege of a [907] free press, with liberty to express our thoughts in a reasonable way, and this advantageous position can be used for the purpose of promoting the entire re-union of Muslim peoples. The True-Believers are scattered all over the world, in the ice-bound land of the white Czar, as well as under the burning sun at the Equator. In the Islands of the West Indies and in British Guiana, in the sandy deserts of Western Australia or the fertile valley of the Nile, the Negro, the Arab, the Indian, the warlike African,

---

225 *TC*, 22/07/1896, pp.892–3.
226 "Giaour" means "infidel".

brave Turk, polite Persian, and the Moor all join in the Fatheha, and turn their face Meccawards five times each twenty-four hours. From Liverpool our steamers and trading vessels journey to each part of the world, and here within the walls of this Institution who knows but that the scattered cords may not be able to be gathered together and woven into a strong rope, *Al-Habbulmateen*, of fraternal union. [...]

This is no idle dream on my part; it is a feasible project, which only requires unity of purpose and effort on the part of True Muslims to be made an accomplished fact. Here in Liverpool, brethren, let us do our part to bring about this glorious consummation of our hopes. 'Tis true that it is not in mortals to command success, but all can work so as to deserve it (applause). Let your fixed determination be to work shoulder to shoulder –

> "Hand to hand united,
> Heart to heart as one"

Always pressing forwards, undaunted by obstacles, not discouraged by no immediate success, working and praying, working and waiting, but always working and striving, having your eyes fixed upon the ultimate goal of your endeavours, THE WORLD FOR ISLAM. Wishing, dreaming, intending, murmuring and repining are all idle and profitless employments. The only manly occupation is to keep doing. The man whose mind is in his work finds his best reward in the work itself. The joy of achievement is vastly beyond the joy of reward. Then let "Onward and upward" be ever your motto and your maxim, "Never say fail." [...] (Loud and continued applause, during which the Sheikh-ul-Islam resumed his seat.) [...] **[908]**[227]

Bro. T. Omar Byrne (hon. sec.) submitted the following report:–
"[...] Mr. McGovern has already dealt with the Wednesday evening lectures, therefore I need only allude to what are popularly known as the "public services." And here I would at once say that a considerable amount of misunderstanding has arisen with regard to these meetings, not only among Christians, but also among some foreign Muslims who have gleaned their knowledge of the meetings second hand, and

227   *TC*, 29/07/1896, pp.905–8.

sometimes not from the best sources. It has been said that these meetings were "Muslim services," and one foolish and ill-informed person
in Egypt[228] went so far as to write a ridiculous book, in which he said
the English Muslims had an organ in their Mosque and used it in their
prayers, and much other nonsense of the same kind. We know that the
writer *never attended a Jumma service at our Mosque.* We also know how,
in what **[919]** manner and in whose company he spent his time in Liverpool,[229] but unfortunately other persons abroad do not know these things,
and therefore it is as well for me to take this opportunity of laying the
correct position of matters before them, and thus endeavour to put a
stop to any wrong impressions upon this subject. These Sunday meetings are not and have never been considered by us as Muslim services, or
used in substitution for the regular prescribed prayers of Islam, neither
are they held in the Mosque, nor is it incumbent upon any True-Believer to attend them unless he or she so desires. They are simply and
only Muslim missionary meetings in the fullest extent of the word, and
are held in the Lecture Hall of the Institution, specially erected for that
purpose. There is no organ in the Mosque, nor is it or has it ever been
used in connection with our prayers. Jumma and every other *Nimaz* in
Liverpool is made exactly in the same manner as it is in every Mosque of
the Hanifee school of Muslims throughout the world. In England Islam
is in its infancy, and it is therefore necessary for us not only to provide
for the religious exercises of our brethren in the faith, but also to conduct an active *propaganda* of our principles. This propaganda or Muslim
missionary work was commenced about nine years ago by our President,
and has been continued ever since. Its success has been remarkable and
gratifying. Without it, it is doubtful if our beloved leader could have
made a dozen converts – through it over one hundred and fifty people
have embraced the faith (applause). Furthermore, what is done is strictly
in conformity with Muslim usage and history, and I boldly assert my firm
conviction that if the Prophet himself (whose name be for ever honoured,
esteemed and blessed), were living in Liverpool today, he would approve
of everything that our president has done with regard to this matter
(applause). I have had the advantage of knowing our president for fully
twenty-five years. I served my apprenticeship in the same office, sitting at
the same desk as he did, and as you all know I have been connected with

---

228 An allusion to Asmay.
229 An allusion to Asmay's association with Keep.

him in business ties from then until now, and after this, the experience of quite a quarter of a century, I unhesitatingly proclaim my belief not only that there is only one God and Mahomed is His prophet, but also that William Henry Abdullah Quilliam has been designated by the Almighty to be "the witness raised up in this land to preach Islam to this people," as referred to in one of the suras of the Koran Shareef (loud and continued applause). Mahomed used to preach Islam in the streets of Mecca and thus secured some of his earlier converts. Here in Liverpool we know that the first converts were obtained by the means of lectures, and when this institution was first formed it was decided to hold a public meeting every Sunday at which an explanatory lecture should be given upon some Islamic subject. Most of the people in this country are Christians, and are accustomed in their churches and chapels to a certain form of service, consisting generally of the singing of a chant, some hymns, the reading of a chapter from the Bible, and a sermon from their clergyman. These people had to be brought gradually into the faith: consequently in order to make them feel more at home at our missionary meetings we held a service something like the one they had been accustomed to in "the days of their ignorance." Instead of their chants in praise of the trinity, the blood-atonement for sins, and such similar foolishness, we opened our meetings with the *Fateha*, rendered into English, and got these enquiring Christians who were feeling their way out of the darkness of their own creed into the light of Islam to join us in piously exclaiming:–

"In the name of God, Merciful, Compassionate!
Praise be to God, the Lord of all that is created,
Thee do we worship, and of Thee do we beg assistance,
Direct us in the right way,
In the way of those to whom Thou has been gracious,
Not of those against whom Thou art incensed,
Nor of those who go astray.
A salamo aliekoum warahmat Allah!"[230] **[923]**

Instead of a chapter from the Bible, we read them a portion of the Koran, and our energetic President compiled a hymn book, in which he placed

---

230 This rendering of the *Fātiḥa*, the preliminary Qur'anic chapter, is placed at the end of the *Collection of Hymns*, p.46, used at the LMI during Sunday services. The final verse ("*A salamo…*") is an addition to the chapter.

many suitable hymns, eliminating objectionable verses from them and making their whole tone Unitarian[231] and Islamic, and to these he added a number of poetical effusions from his own facile pen. In the place of a weary sermon, with its firstly, secondly, and so on, we gave and still give them a lecture upon Islamic history or dogma. We have continued to conduct these meetings in this manner for over nine years, and the results have been most satisfactorily. Many of those who came to deride us have become converts and fervent Muslims. (Applause.) Others openly told us that their previous opinions anent [about] Islam had become considerably changed, and they felt that there was much to be said in our favour. Islam in Liverpool today is respected and honoured by many who nine years ago regarded Moslems as bloodthirsty heathens. (Applause.) Of course the principal figure in this lecturing work has been the Sheikh-ul-Islam of the British Isles.[...] Brother Professor H. Haschem Wilde, Moulvie Mahomed Barakat-Ullah, and Mustapha Khalil have also lectured for us most ably and earnestly, while our brother Professor H. Nasrullah Warren has made an excellent chairman. [...] **[924–5]** [...]

Correspondence

This has been simply enormous during the year. [...] We frequently receive fifty letters in a week and we endeavour to answer them as fully as possible. If it was not for the fact that the Sheikh-ul-Islam dictates most of his replies to two shorthand writers and that we use type-writing machines we could not possibly get through the work. This institution ought to regularly employ a paid clerk, who would, under the supervision of the Sheikh-ul-Islam and the hon. sec., keep all the books, answer all letters, and assist in the sub-editing of the *Crescent* and *Islamic World*. The difficulty, of course, would be first of all to find a suitable man, and, secondly, to provide the funds to pay his wages, During the past year we had to get extra clerical assistance, the details of the cost of which appears

---

231 The Unitarians were an important target group for this Muslim missionary movement. At the fringe of Protestant Nonconformism – they weren't accepted by the National Council of Evangelical Free Churches, their rejection of the Trinity and the divinity of Jesus could make them the most inclined to cross the Rubicon to Islam ("Our Unitarian friends are already two-thirds of the way towards Islam, why not come the other third?", *TC*, 03/06/1893, p.156). However, rejection of Christ as saviour, and therefore of Christianity's purpose, was a larger step than the Muslim converts at the LMI seemed to acknowledge, and Unitarians didn't flock to the LMI to convert.

in the Treasurer's Accounts, and is included under the item of "Printers and other wages" in the balance sheet. If it were not for the fact that our President gives from three to four hours a day out of what should be his leisure time the work could not be grappled with at all. It is not fair to throw all this extra work upon his shoulders, and I for one would like to see a permanent clerk appointed, who could relieve our chief from much of this heavy work (applause). Personally I do what I can, but, as most of you are aware, I was laid aside for seventeen weeks this last year with a serious illness, and prevented from taking as active part as usual in the affairs of the society. I cannot leave this subject without thanking both Mr. McGovern and Professor Wilde for their literary aid with regard to articles and reports for the journals.[232] **[933]**

Our President has alluded to the fact that quotations from our pages frequently appear in foreign newspapers who are on our exchange list. Frequently the source from which they are taken is acknowledged but in many instances they are published without acknowledgment. This is not honest; to boldly appropriate a whole paragraph and pass it off to your readers as original matter is miserable plagiarism, and I trust that those papers who have hitherto done this will refrain from so doing in the future. Our doings have been somewhat extensively noticed in the English press, sometimes favourably, sometimes the reverse. The *Agnostic Journal, Watt's Literary Guide* and the *Freethinker* have all been most fair in the tone of their articles, and it is a pity that some of the Christian press do not take a lesson in politeness and fairness from these papers. The ordinary English secular journals have also as a rule dealt fairly with us, save when they have gone mad upon that convenient bogey, the Armenian question, but the Christian press has, as was quite to be expected, been intolerant, mendacious and unfair. One rampant theological weekly, the *Christian Soldier*, has on several occasions intimated its firm opinion that our President and all of us were doomed to eternal damnation. A local paper called the *Porcupine*, also for some few weeks published a tirade of low, vulgar abuse and scurrility of so gross and contemptible a character as to be simply **[934]** beneath contempt.[233] The proprietors of the journal appear to have recognised this and discharged from their staff all concerned in the publication of these disgraceful articles, appointing a new editor and staff in their place,

232 *TC*, 05/08/1896, pp. 918–19, 923–5.
233 A source quoted by Asmay on the question of Quilliam's financial probity, see Chapter 5.

and since then although the paper has made several references to us, the paragraphs have rather been of a complimentary nature than otherwise. All of the Liverpool daily and weekly newspapers have more or less alluded to our work and given reports of any public meetings we have held, and many kind references to us have appeared in the "Talk in Town" column of the *Liverpool Review*. [...] **[935]**[234]

The Hon. Treasurer (Bro. W. Abdur-Rahman Holehouse) then submitted his report and balance sheet as under:–

1st June 1895, to 31st May 1896,

	£	S.	D.
To Amount presented by the Shahzada on behalf of the Ameer of Afghanistan to the Institution	2500	0	0
To Receipts from all other sources	158	9	2 ½
To Excess of Income over Expenditure, being amounted advanced by Sheikh W. H. Quilliam out of his own pocket to the Institution	191	1?	0 ½
[Total]	£2850	1	3

	£	S.	D.
Expenses of Muslim College, including Masters' Salaries, Stationery, &c., as per detailed account	212	16	9½
Miscellaneous Expenses *re* Mosque, including Gas, Keeper's Wages, Cleaning, &c., as per detailed account	62	14	11

---

234 *TC*, 12/08/1896, pp.933–5.

Expenses of Printing Works, including Printers' Wages, Paper, Postage. Ink, Rent, Cleaning, and other incidental expenses, as per detailed account	429	11	4
Presents to the Ameer and Shahzada, Moulvi Barakat-Ullah and other brethren's' Hotel Bills and general expenses (travelling, &c.), *re* the Shahzada's visit, as per detailed account	193	6	6½
Paid off Mortgage and incidental expenses in connection therewith on premises 11 and 12, Brougham Terrace, as per list	720	0	0
Purchase of 8, Brougham Terrace and incidental expenses in connection therewith (Conveying, Lord of Manor's Fees &c.) as per list	650	15	7
Furniture of Khan, &c., to be founded at 12, Brougham Terrace	57	1	9
Alterations and Repairs at Mosque, including rebuilding Lecture Hall, fitting up Gymnasium, Lavatories, Laboratories, &c., as per detailed list	509	16	4
To Poor, and Distressed Muslims, as per detailed list	13	18	0
[Total]	£2850	1	9

[971] From the above statement it will be seen that about £2,000 (two thousand pounds) of the money so generously presented to the Institution by the Ameer of Afghanistan, has been permanently invested for the benefit of this Institution and the cause of Islam. It will also be noted that the estimates of the committee have been in no case exceeded, and in most instances the expenditure has been less than estimated. The full details of all our receipts and of every penny of this expenditure appear in the books, which are here tonight for any member's inspection. The accounts have been fully audited by Bros. Moulvie Mahomed Barakat-Ullah and

Professor H. Haschem Wilde, the auditors appointed at our last annual meeting, and cross-audited by Messrs. J. H. McGovern, F.L.A.S, and T. C. Davies, in the presence of the Sheikh-ul-Islam, the hon. sec., and the treasurer, the audit lasting nearly a fortnight.

The Auditors' Report

Bro. Moulvie Mahomed Barakat-Ullah said – I have audited most fully and critically the accounts of the Mosque, and seen a voucher for every item of expenditure charged therein. We commenced on the 18th June, and the audit lasted for ten days. Every book kept in connection with the Mosque, the College and Printing Works are produced to us, and we examined them all. The accounts have been kept in a business-like manner, and are quite clear and easy to comprehend, I saw nothing to which the most critical or punctilious person could take exception in the books or accounts. Everything was honest, straight-forward, and above [board], and every assistance was given to the auditors by Sheikh Abdullah Quilliam, the hon. secretary, and the treasurer. (Applause).

Pro. H. Haschem Wilde said – In supplementing the remarks of my co-auditor I desire to say that the fullest possible scrutiny of the accounts of the Mosque has taken place. We have had before us the postage books, in in which is entered every item of postage, including the names and address of each person to whom even a *Crescent* is mailed, the counterfoil receipt books, cash books and ledgers, and everything in connection with the accounts of the Mosque, the School, or the Printing Works. We have seen 1278 vouchers for monies paid. Not an item is down in the books but there is a signed receipt for it. Even when an unpaid or insufficiently stamped letter has come, and 1d. or more has had to be paid as extra postage, then the surcharged wrapper has been preserved and been produced to us. The books contain no less than 35,559 items, and we have checked everything was necessary. I compliment our Institution on the way the books have been kept; they are a credit to the officers who kept them, and the Institution which has such officers. (Applause.) There us, however, in these accounts much food for reflection, and one thing we must seriously take into consideration is the curtailment of some of our expenses. It is not right to expect our President year after year to put his hand in his pocket and advance large sums of money. He works in such a way for Islam as I am sure no other man could or would. No amount of money we could give could repay him for his services, if he ever asked for pay, which I know for one he never will (applause), but to expect him not only to give us so much of his valuable time, and then to expect him also to advance us about £200 a year out of his own pocket, is a great deal too bad. I suggest that our new Executive Committee go very carefully into every item of expenditure in connection with our association, with a view of reducing our expenses as far as possible. (Applause.)

Mr. J. H. McGovern, F.L.A.S., said – Although I was not appointed one of the regular auditors last year, yet at the invitation of the Executive Committee I and Mr. T. C. Davies made an independent and cross-audit of the accounts, the result being that we found everything absolutely and undeniably correct. On behalf of myself and Mr. Davies I confirm all that the two regularly appointed auditors [972] have said. I agree also with Professor Wilde's remarks as to reducing the expenditure where it is possible to do so, and I also think it is not right to expect our President to continue to keep advancing large sums of money to us. I find from the books that since 1887 he has actually lent to the Society the sum of about £1,400, in addition to his gifts and annual subscriptions to the Society. Something ought to be done not only to prevent this happening in the future but also towards raising the money to repay him what he has advanced. (Applause.)

On the motion of Professor Mustapha Khalil Bey, seconded by Professor H. Nasrullah Warren and supported by Bros. Syed Hadi Hassan and A. Hassan Radford, all the reports of the officers and auditors were unanimously adopted with thanks.[235]

The Election of Officers

[...] The meeting then proceeded to the election [987] of the other officers for the Institution, the following being chosen:

Patrons –

His Imperial Majesty Ghazi Abdul-Hamid Khan, Sultan of Turkey, Protector of the Holy Cities, Caliph of the Faithful and Defender of the Faith.

His Majesty Abdur-Rahman Khan, Ameer of Afghanistan, the Lion of the Faith.

---

235 *TC*, 26/08/1896, pp. 970–2.

His Royal Highness Prince Nasrullah Khan, son of the Ameer of Afghanistan.

President –

Sheikh Abdullah Quilliam, Sheikh-ul-Islam of the British Isles. (Unanimously re-elected for the ninth year in succession.)

Honorary Vice-Presidents –

His Excellency Emin Bey, Chamberlain to H.I.M. the Sultan of Turkey.
His Excellency Abdur-Raouf Khan, Khotwal of Cabul.
His Highness the Nawab Hassan Sarwar Jung Bahador of Hyderabad.
His Excellency Sidi Mahomed Torres, Bashador, Morocco.
His Excellency Zekki Pasha, Constantinople.
His Excellency I[brahim] Hakki Bey, Constantinople.
His Excellency Djavid Bey, Caimacan de Cos.
His Excellency General Agha Mirza Mohamed Ali Khan
(Ala-es-Sultaine), Persia.
His Honour Sir Syed Ameer Ali, Judge of the High Court, Calcutta, India.
His Honour Col. Ahmed Bey, Constantinople.
His Honour Mahmoud Essad, Judge of the Tribunal at Smyrna.
His Honour Mahmoud Salem, Judge of the Mixed Tribunal at Egypt.
Professor Mir Aniad Ali, M.A., Dublin University.
His Excellency I. Loutfy Bey, Buda-Pesth.
Mustapha Karsa, Esq., Manchester.
Syed Mahomed Ali, Meerut, India.
A. H. Moolah Dawood, Rangoon, Burmah.
A. H. Musa Khan, Perth, Western Australia.
J. M. H. Gool, Cape Colony.
Peer Mahomed Allarakia, Bombay.
Hajee J. Omar Chamberlain, Transvaal.
Mahomed Sanussi, Sierra Leone.
Yusuffu Shitta Bey, Lagos.

Treasurer –

Bro. W. Abdur-Rahman Holehouse (re-elected).

Hon. Secretary –

Bro. T[homas] Omar Byrne.

Librarian –

Professor H. Nasrullah Warren (re-elected).

Assistant Librarian –

Sister A. Cartwright (re-elected).

Financial Secretary –

Sister L. Hanifa Jones (re-elected).

Committee –

Bros. A. Hassan Radford, J. Omar Quilliam, Alfred Ali Quilliam, and Sister M. A. Lewis.

(The above with the President of the Ladies Committee form the Executive Committee.)
Ladies Committee –

Lady President – Sister H. Khadijah Quilliam-Holehouse; Hon. Secretary – Sister L. H. Jones; Sisters Mrs. Warren, Lewis, Quilliam, and O'Brien, the Misses Cartwright, Warren, and Thomas.

Auditors –

Professors Mustapha Khalil Bey and H. Haschem Wilde.

Hon. Secretaries of the Muslim College –

Messrs. J. Omar Quilliam and J. H. McGovern, F.L.A.S.

Muezzins –

Bros. A. Hassan Radford, R. Ahmed Quilliam Bey, and Billal Quilliam.

The following resolutions were then unanimously passed:–

1. That a Financial Secretary be henceforth annually appointed as an officer of this society with a seat on the Executive Committee.
2. That no person be eligible for the position of an Executive officer of this society who is either under 21 year of age or whose subscription is in arrears.
3. That in future quarterly meetings of members be held for social re-union and discussion.
4. That the suggestions as to home for children made in the President's report be referred to the new Executive for consideration.
5. That the new Executive Committee are requested to economise the expenses so far as is possible without interfering with the efficiency of the Institution. [...] **[988]** [...]
6. I certify the above to be a correct report and full transcript from my shorthand notes of the Annual Meeting of the Liverpool Muslim Institute, held on the 10th day of Muharram, 1314, answering to the date which Christians in error call the 22nd day of June, 1896.

T[homas] Omar Byrne, Hon. Secy.[236]

---

236 *TC*, 02/09/1896, pp.986–8.

SELECT BIOGRAPHIES OF LIVERPOOL MUSLIM INSTITUTE MEMBERS

The following members are either named by Asmay, or were active members of the LMI at the time of his visit.

BARAKATULLAH, Maulana Mahomed (1854–1927)

He was an Indian Islamic scholar trained in Bhopal but linked with the Deoband scholars Mahmudul-Hasan and Ubaydullah Sindhi in later life; a pioneering revolutionary activist in the diaspora whose highly mobile career encompassed British India, London, Paris, Berlin, New York, San Francisco, Tokyo, Kabul, Moscow, and Liverpool; and a leading figure in the militant Ghadar movement that sought to overthrow British rule in India. What linked together the multiple influences on his life – Pan-Islamism, Indian nationalism and communism – was merging the common principles of all three in service of anti-imperialism.[237] At one point he served as the Prime Minister of the Provisional Azad Hind (Free India) Government based in Kabul.

He came to Britain in 1887 and worked in London as a private tutor in Persian, Arabic and Urdu; a young Maulana Mohamed Ali Jauhar (1878–1931) was among his tutees. He came to Liverpool penniless in 1893, according to Asmay's account, and chiefly worked as Quilliam's secretary, but also served as an imam and taught at the Institute. In 1894, after Quilliam's return from Lagos, Barakatullah proposed that Quilliam be named Sheikh-ul-Islam of the British Isles at a special meeting of the LMI; the proposal was passed by an unanimous vote of the membership.[238] In 1895, Barakatullah was able to make a connection to the Afghan court

237 M.A. Khan, 'Universal Islam: the faith and political ideologies of Maulana Barakatullah Bhopali', *Sikh Formations*, 10/1, 2014, pp.57–67, DOI: 10.1080/17448727.2014.888246.

238 'A Manx Chief of Islam', *Mona's Herald*, 10/10/1894, p.5.

during the visit of Crown Prince Nasrullah Khan to Liverpool, which was politically significant as Afghanistan later supported the Ghadar movement. After criticising Quilliam and his mismanagements to Asmay in private correspondence that was later published, Barakatullah nonetheless played a role in the Institute until he left London in 1896, after assisting in the financial audit for the Institute's AGM that year.

BYRNE, Thomas (Omar) (1856–1901)

He was a legal clerk, the son of working-class Irish Catholic immigrants to Liverpool. Before joining the LMI, he received a Jesuit education, and had considered entering the priesthood. At fifteen, he entered a solicitor's office, where he met the young William Quilliam, aged seventeen. With Byrne in Kensington and Quilliam in Fairfield, they were neighbours and became friends. When Quilliam started his own firm, Thomas joined him before going to London to work for the pro-Home Rule Irish Parliamentary Party, eventually campaigning for an Irish constituency in Parliament. Byrne then returned to Liverpool to pursue a career as a professional shorthand writer and journalist. He reconnected with Quilliam in 1887 while covering his lecture on "Fanatics and Fanaticism" at Vernon Hall. This lecture was Quilliam's first attempt to present Islam in an indirect manner, gaining his first three converts[239] and leading to Quilliam's boycott by Liverpool's Temperance societies. Byrne's interest was piqued, and he started attending the LMI meetings, converting to Islam in 1889.

At Brougham Terrace, Byrne acted as the LMI's librarian and presided over the Wednesday Literary and Debating Society. In the aftermath of Asmay's visit in 1895, he was appointed Hon. Secretary of the Institute. At the following Annual Meeting, he presented an *apologia* of the LMI's works and internal affairs, defending the Sunday "public services" and brushing off Asmay's pamphlet as "a ridiculous book" by "one foolish and ill-informed person in Egypt".[240] As one of the more confident writers at the Institute, he often penned letters and refutations to the press, signing as "Hon. Secretary to the United English Muslim Societies". In 1896, he began compiling a history of Islam in England, but was unable to complete it due to ill-health. Unable to work, he was asked by Quilliam

---

239 In order of conversion: James Ali Hamilton (d. 1899), Elizabeth Fatima Cates (d. 1900) and David Dawood Grundy (d. 1891).

240 See Appendix 2.

to sub-edit *The Crescent.*

He died unmarried at the age of forty-five. He was buried with Islamic rites in the Nonconformist section of the West Derby Cemetery, the funeral service being led by Abdullah Quilliam.

CUSS, George Francis (1844–94)

He was born into an Anglican family, but preferred to question the faith and tenets of the Church of England, becoming an agnostic. He worked as an innkeeper in Manchester but thereafter became a teetotaller. Upon moving to Liverpool, he met William Quilliam and converted to Islam from agnosticism (the only LMI member recorded as doing so[241]), becoming in 1891 an important member of the young group of converts. As a teetotaller, he managed a temperance hotel on Camden Street, Liverpool. In 1891, while serving as an elected "auditor" at the LMI,[242] his wife, Eliza, was found guilty of managing a brothel at the hotel and was fined (he was found guilty of the same offence in 1892). In 1892, his wife was found guilty of perverting the course of justice by bribing a witness in another brothel-keeping case and was imprisoned. According to Asmay, it was commonly related in Liverpool in 1895 that William Quilliam owned the hotel that the Cuss couple managed on his behalf but he had managed not to get charged at the time.[243] Cuss left the Liverpool Muslim Institute and Liverpool in 1892, moving with his wife to Southampton where he opened another alcohol-free public house. He died in April 1894, three months after his wife, and was buried in unconsecrated grounds.

HOLEHOUSE née BURROWS, Harriet (Khadijah) Quilliam- (1832–1901)

She was William Abdullah Quilliam's mother, the daughter of Dr John Bamford Burrows (1799–1882), Methodist surgeon and teetotaller from Cheshire, later a leader of the United Methodist Free Churches, a breakaway from the Wesleyans.[244] Harriet travelled with young William to Europe, and it is claimed later travelled widely to Algeria, Malta and Turkey. She was a social activist and served as the honorary secretary of the local branch of Josephine Butler's famous Ladies National

---

241 *TC*, 20/11/1907, p.332.
242 Monro, p.7.
243 See a full discussion of the court cases in the Introduction.
244 *LM*, 06/07/1882, p.5

Association for the Repeal of the Contagious Diseases Acts, while her father was vice-president of the local branch of the same Association.[245] The Acts sought to reduce venereal disease in the armed forces. Police were allowed to arrest women living in ports and military towns who they believed were prostitutes and force them to be examined for venereal disease. Butler toured the country making speeches calling for their repeal. Prior to this campaign, Butler had set up philanthropic hostels to care for prostitutes stricken with venereal disease. Through this activism, Harriet and her son William, then a teenager, were exposed to Butler's arguments about the sexual double standard and the iniquitous treatment of distraught women, and to her use of scripture to challenge the Church's treatment of women.[246] Like her father, Harriet was a Good Templar from 1872 and was appointed Grand Worthy Vice-Templar of England.

Harriet converted to Islam in 1893 on the day of William Quilliam's birthday. Jokingly, she alluded to her conversion as her birthday gift to him.[247] She affixed her name to the LMI "Allegiance book", taking the name Khadijah. She served as President of the LMI's Ladies Committee. As testament to a certain religious fluidity, allowing LMI members to maintain both an attachment to Christian cultural identity and allegiance to the Islamic faith, Quilliam reports that his dying mother, a week before her death, "recited with holy fervour to her son the first four verses of the 23rd Psalm, attributed to the prophet Sidna Dawood".[248]

Harriet lived close to her only son on their family estate in Fairfield Crescent. When her husband, Robert Quilliam, died in 1889, she stayed with Quilliam in Prospect Vale, Fairfield, before marrying William Holehouse, an LMI member, a year later. She was buried at St James cemetery, next to her first husband Robert Quilliam.

HOLEHOUSE, William (Abdur-Rahman)

He was Quilliam's stepfather, the second husband of Harriet Quilliam. Holehouse was an important figure at the time of Asmay's visit, the LMI

---

245 *LM*, 15/11/1871, p.6; *TC*, 17//04/1901, p.243. Samuel Quilliam, William's paternal grandfather, also supported the campaign against the CD Acts.

246 "In the Bible I find the labourer deprived of just wages, the wronged widow, the neglected orphan, the leper driven out of society… Their cry, it is said, enters into the ears of God." See J. Butler (ed.), *Woman's Work and Women's Culture* (London, MacMillan, 1869), p.x.

247 *TC*, 12/04/1901, p.260.

248 *TC*, 17//04/1901, p.244.

treasurer, and he oversaw the refurbishment of the mosque-cum-lecture hall funded by Nasrullah Khan and used for most social and religious events held at the LMI. His interests were not solely religious: one of his lectures given at the Literary and Debating Society being "Which part of the World Produces the Most Beautiful Women". According to Asmay, he acted as Quilliam's enforcer, "kicking her [Nafeesa Keep] out of the publishing house because she was informing Muslims in the Orient about their doings." After Quilliam's mother's death in 1901, he is no longer mentioned in *The Crescent*.

JEFFERY, James Bartholomew (Djamel ud-Din Bokhari) (1830–1905)

Like many of his fellow convert members of the LMI, he was a working man, employing up to twenty men in his plumbing and decorating business. He was a member of the Orange Loyal Protestant order and was appointed a Grand Lodge Officer at the age of twenty-four. He co-founded the Liverpool Working Men's Conservative Association in 1866, which went on to cement Tory political domination in the city for decades under the leadership of Sir Archibald Salvage. In 1873, he met William Quilliam, who had joined the Association, and may have acted as a political mentor to the younger Quilliam. From 1870 he was initiated into the Ancient Order of Freemasons and was made Knight of Constantinople. In 1874 he was initiated into Quilliam's own fringe Freemasonry order, the Ancient Order of the Zuzimites, becoming in 1884 the order's "Most Worshipful Grand Treasurer".[249] He was also a leading member of one of the largest fraternal organisations in England, the Royal Antediluvian Order of Buffaloes. Strongly attached to the Evangelist Low-Church, he maintained an interest in his friend's conversion to Islam and missionary efforts, but "simply attended the meetings out of sympathy".[250] In 1889, however, he witnessed pro-Christian violence against the converts at the Liverpool Muslim lecture hall and joined forces with the converts to expel the ruffians. According to *The Crescent*, he was so appalled by the attacks that he chose to convert to Islam, rising

---

249 For more on the Zuzimites and Quilliam's involvement with fringe Masonry, see P.D. Bowen, "Abdullah Quilliam and the Rise of International Esoteric-Masonic Islamophilia" in Gilham and Geaves (eds), *Victorian Muslim*, pp.25–39,154–161.
250 *IW*, 6/63, p.55; *TC*, 02/09/1903, p.155.

to pronounce the *shahāda*,[251] taking the name Djemal ud-deen Barakat, then Bokhari from 1897. At the Liverpool Muslim Institute, he acted as librarian, lecturer for the Literary and Debating Society, committee member for the Medina Home for Children, and organiser of important social events such as the Muslim annual picnics. He also replaced Quilliam in conducting the "*Jumma*" prayers at the Mosque. By the time of his conversion, he was living in Everton, West Derby, like other pivotal converts Nasrullah and Rosa Warren and Haschem Wilde.

Jeffery considered himself a devout Muslim and follower of Quilliam, expressing respect for the Prophet and the Sultan, and hoped to visit Constantinople and perform the pilgrimage to Mecca.[252] According to his obituary in *The Crescent*, sensing that his end was near, Jeffery produced a written statement in which he desired that "no Christian service is to read over [him]" and that he be "interred as a Muslim". He died of a heart attack, reportedly with the printed notes of his last lecture on "Idolatry in Christianity" by his side. His family did not honour his request and so he was buried in 1903 in the Anglican section of Anfield Cemetery. Nevertheless, Quilliam performed the *janāza* prayer, in the company of convert members of the LMI and of the Zuzimite Order.[253]

KEEP, née Klamroth, Mary Theresa (Nafeesa) (1844–1925)

Born in Indiana, USA, Keep lost her parents at an early age and was raised by her uncle's multi-confessional family. Keep was an American journalist, divorced from a wealthy New York newspaper owner and Wall Street speculator Charles Dwight Keep, whom she had married in a Catholic Church in 1872. Before the latter's death in 1887, she spent two years as a special correspondent in Paris (1882–4) and was described as a "well-known woman in newspaper row".[254] Although "Charley" Keep was ill-tempered and led a dissolute life, Keep maintained that she had been coerced into

---

251 The story of Jeffery's conversion, as it is related in *The Crescent* and *The Islamic World*, draws an obvious parallel with the conversion of Hamza, the Prophet Muhammad's uncle, who converted after the former was attacked by Abu Jahl. "Brother Jeffery, who was present, seized the ringleader of this band of Christian desperadoes just as he was about to fling half a brick at the Sheikh" (*IW, idem*). By connecting these two conversion narratives, the aim was to associate the genesis of the LMI with the birth of Islam, and Quilliam's role as analogous to the Prophet's, in order to legitimise the LMI and its leader in the eyes of Muslim subscribers and donators.

252 *TC*, 06/09/1899, p.150.

253 *TC*, 02/09/1903, p.157.

254 *The Boston Globe*, 10/06/1887, p.4.

accepting the divorce. It appears that Charles had been living with another woman, the cook of railroad magnate and speculator Jay Gould, with whom he had already had five children by the time of his divorce with Mary in 1884, Mary having left New York for France. Keep was convinced that her former husband, Charles, his new wife Bridget McMahon and his business associate, Cuthbert Mills, had conspired together to deprive her of the money she had given Charles to start a newspaper, *The Wall Street News*. She intended to sue Charles for this money and apply for an annulment of her divorce and reinstate an earlier will that favoured her instead of a later one favouring Bridget McMahon when he died. Charles' untimely death did not deter Keep, as she was convinced that her husband was either still alive or had been murdered by the McMahon family and Cuthbert Mills to gain control of the newspaper, valued at $500,000. Keep successfully appealed and witnessed Charles' grave being dug up. Recognising Charles' body, she asked for the corpse to be kept in a receiving vault so that she could appeal to the Monmouth County (New Jersey) coroner and district attorney to assess it for evidence of foul play. It was reported that, "[i]mmediately afterwards Mrs. Keep fainted, and remained unconscious for some time."[255] There was negative press over her legal quest for a divorce annulment, including a row with a Catholic priest who had refused to perform mass over her ex-husband's corpse as a divorcee. Keep was left fortuneless and bitterly distrustful of a system that had, for her, contributed to and validated her marginalisation. It is very important to note that Webb, Quilliam and Asmay all took her version of events before and after her divorce at face value.

Keep got involved with the American section of the Theosophical Society in Brooklyn, led by William Quan Judge, who had founded the international movement with H.P. Blavatsky and Henry S. Olcott in 1875. Keep contributed papers to *The Path*, its official organ. In March 1893, Muhammad Alexander Russell Webb, a leading American Muslim convert and theosophist, was invited by the Society to give a lecture on Islam. Shortly after, Keep left her occupation at the Theosophical Society to be hired by Webb as secretary of the Moslem World Publishing Company, secretary of the American Islamic Propaganda, and editor-in-chief for *The Voice of Islam*. Meanwhile, William Q. Judge was accused by Olcroft and Blavatsly's successor Annie Besant of fraud by forging names and handwriting in letters, his involvement in the scandal dating from

255 *Indianapolis Journal*, 17/01/1888, p.1; 18/01/1888, p.2.

155

the time when Keep was still employed as a writer on *The Path*.

At the American Islamic Propaganda, Keep developed a sense of social reform, justice and gender equality that she associated with Islam and the Islamic world. She read Charles Hamilton's translation of the *Hedaya*, a medieval Hanafi *fiqh* compendium used in translation as the key reference for Anglo-Muhammadan law in British India, that convinced her of the benefits of a Sunni orthodox system of social organisation. A year later, she engaged in a severe dispute over Webb's mismanagement of his movement and accused him of embezzling funds received from foreign donors, reporting Webb to the Ottoman Consul in New York, Ismael Bey.

In September 1894, two new rival American organisations, one led by E. Nabokoff, and the other by J.A. Lant and A.L. Rawson, were created to counter Webb's leadership. Nafeesa Keep decided to pursue efforts to create another Islamic movement. She sailed for Liverpool in February 1895, from where she intended to reach India "in pursuit of the religion that had captivated her, ... to return [to America] as its accredited and trusted evangelist."[256] Arriving in Liverpool, she visited the LMI the following day for the "*Jumma Namaz*". She was welcomed and later employed by Quilliam as co-editor for *The Crescent*, when her money ran out. At the LMI, she made the argument "to convince English ladies that the statements usually made to the position of women in Islam are incorrect", and that "Mohammedan women ... are much happier than their Western sisters."[257] Having been left fortuneless, as first spouse, in favour of her former husband's second wife and offspring, she had developed the idea that Islamic societies, and rules of inheritance, would have been favourable to her and for women in general.[258] She became a prominent figure at the LMI, accepting the role of assistant superintendent for the new Muslim College for children. Very soon, however, Keep made very similar accusations of fraud and embezzlement towards Quilliam that she had raised against Webb. Furthermore, she didn't identify with the convert members of the LMI who, according to letters she wrote to Turkish Sultan Abdulhamid[259] and Afghan Prince Nasrullah Khan, had not adopted orthodox Islamic mores and religious practices. She found in the

---

256 *The Courier-Journal (Louisville)*, 31/12/1899, p.15.
257 *LM*, 12/02/1895, p.6.
258 Her first lecture at the LMI, "Women Under the Islamic Law", was published in *IW*, March 1895, pp.342–51.
259 See Appendix 1.

Turkish Cairo resident and journalist Samih Yusuf Asmay, who arrived in Liverpool in August 1895 to investigate the LMI, an ideal confidant and ally. Via the Liverpool consul, Keep appealed for financial help to relocate to an Islamic country, but her pleas were rejected. Keep was expelled from the LMI, and thrown out of the Crescent Publishing Company offices by Quilliam's father-in-law, according to Asmay.

Keep moved to London where she worked as a freelance journalist, meeting a wealthy Egyptian who invited her to Cairo to act as English instructor to his child. In Cairo, she met Mohammed Dollie, who had recently established a mosque in London. They agreed to join forces so that she would tour Muslim countries to appeal for funds to establish a Muslim colony in the USA, an ambitious scheme that did not go anywhere.

Back in London, where she joined Dollie's community, she then decided in 1901 to relocate to Perth, Australia,[260] where she qualified as a nurse and from 1906 took an active part in advocating women's involvement in Australian politics. She died in 1925 and was buried in Anglican grounds.

RADFORD, Arthur (Hassan) (1861–1918)

Arthur Hassan Radford was raised as an Anglican, but later joined the newly created Salvation Army. He trained as a plumber and travelled overseas, where he might have gained some knowledge of Arabic, referring in his lecture at the LMI "to his experience in foreign lands, and his views regarding the beauty and adaptability of the Islamic form of worship".[261] In 1890, after having been baptised into the Catholic faith, Radford converted to Islam at the LMI, becoming "one of the earliest English converts to Islam".[262] He was most likely practising both Christian and Muslim faiths for at least the first year following his conversion: when the LMI was visited in 1891 by a critical missionary, the latter noted that "some days after [he] found [Radford] professing penitence and seeking admission into the Christian Church".[263] In Liverpool he continued to work as a plumber and became the first official muezzin at the LMI, calling to prayer from the museum room window out to the

---

260 Whether she went to connect with its Afghan Muslim community led by Anglophile Hassan Musa Khan is currently undetermined. As Khan was in contact with the LMI during Keep's time there, it is reasonable to assume she was aware of this community.

261 *TC*, 21/08/1895, p.121.

262 *TC*, 18/07/1900, p.36.

263 Monro, pp.16–17.

West Derby Road every Friday and Sunday, and every evening during Ramadan. The few lectures he gave for the LMI Literary and Debating Society indicate his concern with worker rights: "voters have it in their power to remedy the existing evils which Free Trade has brought upon the working classes in the United Kingdom; this remedy must be applied through the political party which proves itself the friend of the working people."[264] After December 1900, he is no longer mentioned in either *The Crescent* or *The Islamic World*. The most regularly appointed muezzins thereafter were Mahomed Abdul-Latif (1903–6) and Ahmed C. Brann (1906–8). Hassan Radford died in Liverpool, aged 57, and was buried in consecrated grounds at Anfield Cemetery.

QUILLIAM, Mary Ann Lyon (1864–1952)

She was the mother of William Quilliam's children, Ethel Miriam (b. 1885), Mohamed Henry (b. 1886), Lillian Ayesha (b. 1887), Florence Zuleika (b. 1890) and May Habeeba (b. 1897). Mary met Quilliam while she was a singer at the Liverpool Theatre.[265] By 1885, before the birth of their first child, they were already sharing a terraced house in Lombard Street, a five-minute walk from the house at Brougham Terrace that Quilliam would purchase for his burgeoning group of converts. After the birth of Mohamed Henry, Lillian and Florence, the couple moved to Saxony Road, also near to the LMI, while his other wife Hannah resided at Fairfield Crescent, West Derby, with other Quilliam family members. By 1901, they were residing at 42 Rufford Road, West Derby, a mere five-minute walk from Quilliam's official abode with Hannah. Both wives were therefore close neighbours for a time.

Although, according to Asmay, Mary and Hannah "[could not] stand to see each other's faces out of intense jealousy", their children freely mingled at the LMI, and it was not unknown for them to appear together on official occasions at the Institute. In 1895, both Hannah and Mary were part of the reception for the Crown Prince Nasrullah Khan when he visited the mosque. There is a photograph that possibly depicts both wives and their children with Quilliam and other LMI members in a group portrait.

Although not married to Quilliam by common law, the 1901 Census lists Mary as Quilliam, which shows that she considered herself as

---

264 "Free Trade and Fair Trade", *TC*, 10/07/1895, p.23.
265 Geaves, *Islam in Victorian Britain*, p.53.

legitimate a wife as Hannah. To avoid suspicions of bigamy, the identity William gives is "Henry M. Quilliam, journalist and author". The choice of this pseudonym lends further credence to the theory that the mysterious "Henri Marcel/Mustapha Léon" writing for *The Crescent* was one of Quilliam's pennames, and a way of alluding to his second wife's maiden name (Leon/Lyon). One possible reason for Quilliam's more prominent promotion of the Leon identity ca. 1900 was because of the greater pressure that Mary was putting on him to legitimise their marriage. One indication of this is the witnessed memorial to their Islamic marriage that he submitted to the Ottoman authorities in May 1900, which claimed that he and Mary had married as believing Muslims on 23 September 1883 (Quilliam only converted privately three years later in 1886).[266]

Mary married Quilliam in Preston Registry Office in December 1909, after Hannah's death. Now finally his wife by common law after many years of waiting, Quilliam did not share a household with her as a legally married couple. He had left her for Edith Miriam Spray, a convert, living under the false identities of Henri Marcel Léon and Edith de Léon (ironically, the same name Quilliam had coined with Mary Lyon in order for them to live *incognito*). Both Mary and Edith were present at Quilliam's funeral in 1932. Mary, like Quilliam's first official wife Hannah, did not convert to Islam, remaining a Christian until her death in 1952.[267] None of her children remained professing Muslims.

WARREN, Henry (Nasrullah) Nevil Cromwell (1866–1930)

His father was an officer of Inland Revenue and a Unitarian, who died in 1882. His mother, Elizabeth, did not remarry. Henry converted to Islam in 1890, after having been invited by his mother to attend a series of public lectures given during the Sunday services at the Liverpool Muslim Institute. His mother and sister Rosa also converted and became active members of the LMI.

From 1895 he gave chemistry, electricity and metallurgy classes to the pupils of the Muslim College and two Tuesday evening classes, on chemistry and electricity, at the LMI. He also gave science lectures at the Wednesday Literary and Debating Society meetings. He was also keen

---

266 Y. PRK. A. Dosya 12, Gömlek 54, Tarih 1314 C 25, cited in M.A. Sherif, "A Forgotten Memorial from Abdullah and Mariam Quilliam to the Ottoman Sheikh-ul-Islam", *Islamic Review (Special Issue)*, 2018, pp.34–5, 62–3.

267 Gilham, *Loyal Enemies*, p.120.

on demonstrating how science could account for paranormal phenomena and Spiritualism. At the time of Asmay's visit in 1895, he acted as LMI Librarian and had paid two visits, with Barakatullah and Quilliam, to the Crown Prince of Afghanistan Nasrullah Khan in London, who had donated £2500 to the LMI towards a purpose-built mosque. There, he gifted the Crown Prince a hat pin that could light up, which he had specially commissioned. When their convert mother, who had taken the name of Leylah, died in December 1899, Henry and Rosa moved to St Domingo Road, Henry keeping on the place in Albion Street as a laboratory. He regularly advertised his business in *The Crescent*, a research laboratory on 18 Albion Street which sold the "Boron Carbon Battery".

Quilliam and Warren were close associates in faith. In 1899, they both visited a synagogue to attend a special choral in aid of the Liverpool Hebrew Philanthropic Society.[268] Also, Quilliam would call on Warren to act as an expert witness in chemistry at Quilliam's behest to support his clients' claims in court.[269] Despite Nasrullah's strong involvement with Quilliam and his Institute, with the closing of the Muslim College in October 1902 his name ceases to appear in *The Crescent*.

WARREN, Rosa Elizabeth Augusta (1862–1925)

Born in West Derby, she converted in 1890 at the same as her brother Henry Nasrullah and her mother Elizabeth Leylah. Rosa lived with her brother at 131 Domingo Road, Everton. She was a piano and dance teacher and acted as organist at the LMI Sunday mission services. According to Yusuf Samih Asmay, she was "young", and he found her "somewhat pretty and nonchalant".

Rosa took part in the celebrations at the LMI, often playing music for the guests. On public Christmas events[270] or for the Eid al-Adha ("Bairam Kebir") festival[271] at the LMI she entertained the audience by playing the zither, the Bell harp or the mandolin. She was on the board of the Medina Home for Children, the governing committee which was presided over by Haschem Wilde. As a committee member of the Literary and Debating Society, her contributions revolved around music and dance

268 *LM*, 20/11/1899, p.9.
269 *The Guardian*, 22/02/1901, p.10.
270 *TC*, 02/01/1895, p.3.
271 *TC*, 19/05/1897, p.316.

("Dancing: Ancient and Modern")[272] or touched on other topics of general interest ("Curious Epitaphs: What the Living Think of the Dead").[273]

When her lodger and music-hall partner, ex-LMI member Hedley Wilde, died suddenly and mysteriously in 1912, Rosa came forward as his wife to make a legal claim to an amount of money that had been stolen from him and to his property deeds. Rosa lived at the family home in Everton until her death in 1924, aged 60. She was buried in a consecrated section of Kirkdale cemetery.

WILDE, Hedley (Haschem) (1870–1912)

Raised in Everton in a family of esteemed Evangelical Anglicans, he secured a diploma from the National Council of Education before considering whether to enter the Christian ministry. Under the auspices of a local clergyman, Wilde engaged in theological study but disliked the imposed curriculum and not being allowed to investigate alternative viewpoints through independent study. Wilde was about to enter St Aidan's College, Birkenhead, when his parents decided that he should attend St. Bee's instead due to its clearer evangelical ethos. Taken aback by the divisions and controversies between the High and Low Church, Wilde abandoned the idea of entering the ministry. Instead, while remaining a regular churchgoer and Sunday-school teacher, he engaged in study of the Scriptures, which led him to doubt Anglican liturgy and then, more generally, the doctrines of Christianity. Wilde's published articles and lectures at the LMI reflect a strong aversion to Christianity, a tendency that Yusuf Samih Asmay criticises. According to a profile of Wilde in *The Crescent*, which could embellish in furtherance of its anti-Christian rhetoric, he was requested by the parson to stop teaching Bible class "as he was teaching nothing else than pure Unitarianism". Wilde started to explore other Christian denominations, "seeking truth and finding none," before losing hope, "preferring to worship the God of Nature in his heart".

In 1892, he applied for the position of assistant master at the Liverpool Muslim College and, after eighteen months of lengthy discussions with Abdullah Quilliam and other Muslims from the LMI, converted, openly proclaiming his new faith, being known as "Haschem" in *The Crescent* from January 1893. When Hugh Yehiya Johnson left Liverpool

272 *TC*, 07/12/1898, p.337.
273 *TC*, 29/03/1899, p.201.

for Egypt, Wilde replaced him as headmaster of the Liverpool Muslim College. He also occupied numerous functions at the LMI as Auditor, Secretary, Treasurer, Vice-President of the Institute and President of the Debating Society. As Asmay notes in 1895, his contributions to the Sunday service speeches were shockingly anti-Christian, seven of the fourteen Sunday speeches he gave from July 1895 to 1896 aimed to promote the Islamic faith by directly refuting Christianity. Wilde remained a bachelor during his LMI years, lodging with siblings Rosa and Henry Nasrallah Warren at their home on St Domingo Road, Everton. Wilde was a calm, unobtrusive personality, suffering from poor health, who had refrained from alcohol all his life. When Henry Nasrullah Warren married in 1901, Haschem and Rosa Warren left the Warrens' home, an event that coincided with his name no longer appearing on the lists of committee members at the LMI.

After 1908, Henry Warren's divorce and the demise of Quilliam and the LMI, Wilde returned to live with the Warrens, pursuing a music-hall career and living off lands he owned in Macclesfield, Wales. In 1912 he won £1500 in a lawsuit regarding some property but the money was later stolen from him. He headed to a public house in Flydden, Flintshire, to drown his sorrows in whisky, remarking to the innkeeper that "it was his first that day and would be his last". The following day he was found dead in an empty house in Flydden from heart failure. Identifying as his wife and music-hall partner, ex-LMI member Rosa Warren travelled up with her brother Henry to identify the body. She claimed that although she did not know the names of Wilde's solicitors, and for that reason could not access Wilde's property deeds, "she was led to understand that if anything happened to him, the money would be left to her".[274]

---

274 *The Guardian*, 06/01/1912, p.11.